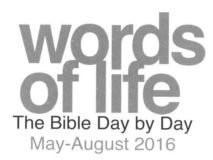

words of life

The Bible Day by Day

May-August 2016

ISBN 978-1-911149-00-2
e-book ISBN 978-1-911149-01-9

A catalogue record for this book is available from the British Library

Writer: Major Beverly Ivany
Project editors: Major Trevor Howes, and Paul Mortlock
Cover design: Jooles Tostevin

Unless indicated otherwise, Scripture quotations are taken from
The Holy Bible, New International Version–UK.
Copyright © 1979, 1984 by Biblica, formerly International Bible Society.
Anglicised edition first published in Great Britain in 1979
by Hodder & Stoughton, an Hachette UK company.
Used by permission. All rights reserved.

The Salvation Army policy is to use papers that are natural, renewable
and recyclable products and made from wood grown in sustainable forests.
The logging and manufacturing processes are expected to conform to
the environmental regulations of the country of origin.

Published by Salvation Books
The Salvation Army International Headquarters
101 Queen Victoria Street, London EC4V 4EH, United Kingdom

www.salvationarmy.org

Printed and bound in the UK by Page Bros Ltd, Norwich NR6 6SA

Contents

Abbreviations

From the writer of *Words of Life*

The Purpose of Prayer

Greetings in the name of the Lord Jesus Christ! It is wonderful to reach out to fellow believers from all around the world by means of this devotional book, *Words of Life*. This year we are focusing on prayer, and in this edition 'The Purpose of Prayer'.

Why do we pray as Christians? Simply because it's expected of us? Could it ever become routine, a ritual? Or do we *enjoy* our time in prayer? I feel there is something inborn within us all that longs to commune with our Creator; to spend quality time in prayer, because somehow the connection made with Holy God brings so much strength, comfort, encouragement and, yes, even healing.

In the Old Testament, prayer was essential for God's people. We will see in 1 and 2 Kings how the Children of Israel did well when their leader, and the people themselves, took everything to God in prayer. But when prayer ceased, everything went wrong – and the people were left distraught. Yet people such as the prophets Elijah and Elisha came along to encourage the Israelites once again and to show them the great purpose in bringing *everything* to God in prayer. Nehemiah was also a tremendous man of faith and prayer – helping his people restore *their* prayer life. And Solomon saw immense purpose in prayer – especially as in Ecclesiastes he questioned the meaning of life.

In the New Testament we witness the prayer life of Jesus in Mark's Gospel and the middle section of the Gospel of John. In Paul's powerful Letter to the Romans we observe how the apostle relied heavily upon prayer – to help spread the gospel, reaching out to affirm the believer's faith in the Lord, and even to sustain himself through many trials and sufferings.

On the weekends we have a psalm or proverb, and also a song for meditation and reflection. Prayer overrides these readings, for prayer opens up revelations not seen before in God's Word and through the words of the hymns. This edition also has reflections on The Salvation Army's *Boundless* Congress of 2015; and our guest writer of a meaningful Pentecost series is Major Florence Pamacheche from Zimbabwe.

May the Lord stir our hearts, once again, as we dwell on the purpose of prayer for our own lives – and for the lives of those God brings into our sphere of influence. To God be the glory!

Beverly A. Ivany
Toronto, Canada

Be Thou my Vision

Where there is no vision [no redemptive revelation of God] the people perish (v 18 AB).

Our hymn for today is an old Irish song in both text and tune. It was translated into English in the early part of the 20th century, but probably dates back as early as the 8th century. It is a plea for God to establish himself as our chief object of worship and desire – for he alone is Sovereign. He is Lord of my heart and yours:

> Be thou my vision, O Lord of my heart!
> Naught be all else to me, save that thou art;
> Thou my best thought in the day and the night,
> Waking or sleeping, thy presence my light.
> (SASB 573 v 1)

Vision is a key word for today's world. We all need vision to see what lays ahead in our spiritual journey, to make life the best it can be for all concerned. But we also need *wisdom* in making right decisions, and for discerning what God wants for each one of us:

> Be thou my wisdom, be thou my true word;
> I ever with thee and thou with me, Lord;
> Thou my great Father and I thy true son;
> Thou in me dwelling and I with thee one.
> (v 2)

The song reminds us that our treasure is not found in earthly things, but in God alone; it then ends with praising God as our High King – to be worshipped as Ruler and Lord. As we sing this final verse, joining our voices with those around the world, may God give us the *vision* to see the world as God would have it be:

> High King of Heaven, thou Heaven's bright Sun,
> Grant me its joys after victory is won!
> Christ of my own heart, whatever befall,
> Still be my vision, O Ruler of all!

A New King

'As the LORD was with my lord the king, so may he be with Solomon to make his throne even greater than the throne of my lord King David!' (v 37).

As we commence the Book of 1 Kings, we soon note that the golden era of King David's reign is coming to an end – as his own life ends. His son, Solomon, prepares to take the throne. He has been given his father's dream of building a temple in Jerusalem, but before long he begins to lack the same passion for God as David possessed. Solomon developed a divided heart and, eventually, a divided kingdom.

The opening chapter sees another of David's sons, Adonijah, trying to take the throne for himself. Bathsheba approaches David, her husband – begging him to declare Solomon as king. David makes his desire known to her:

'Solomon your son shall be king after me, and he will sit on my throne in my place' (v 30).

A new king; all part of God's divine plan. David had reigned for 40 years. Not perfectly – as we well know – but he had a deep love for God and a strong passion to rule his people well. Now Solomon was to rule. I am sure David prayed that his son would *also* keep very close to the Lord.

We pray for our children's well-being; that they will follow the Lord's direction in life. If we don't have children, we no doubt pray for young adults – that they will look to God for purpose and meaning. And if they are *not* following God's lead, we pray they soon will. Let us take time, right now to present them before the Lord.

PRAYER

Lord, as David prayed for his son, we bring before you our sons and daughters, and all young adults – asking that they be drawn close to you. Protect them. May they become aware of your guarding presence and accept your loving guidance now, and always.

Called and Commissioned

'So be strong … observe what the LORD your God requires: Walk in his ways' (vv 2-3).

Sometimes people get the idea that only Salvation Army officers or church clergy are called and commissioned by God. Not true! We are *all* called and we're *all* commissioned to go into the world and spread the good news of the gospel.

King David knew Solomon was called and chosen by God to succeed him. And so, after publicly declaring his son to be his successor, he commissioned and charged Solomon to be worthy of his high calling. If Solomon proved to be true to the Lord, then God promised David the following, which he shared with his son:

"'If your descendants watch how they live, and if they walk faithfully before me with all their heart and soul, you will never fail to have a man on the throne of Israel'" (v 4).

All the new king needed to do was follow in the ways of the Lord; to be obedient to him. Clear-cut? Yes. Easy to do? Not always – for we are human. We fail. Temptations come to us and we let God down. Challenges happen along the way, often unexpectedly – messing us up and getting us off track. We are confused, troubled. We become frightened and not sure what to do next.

Author Max Lucado responds: 'You'll get through this. It won't be painless. It won't be quick. But God will use this mess for good. Don't be foolish or naïve. But don't despair either. With God's help, you'll get through this.'[1]

No matter what we are facing at present or what lies ahead of us, we need to remember God is with us all the way. After all, we are *called* by God to be his servants. And we are *commissioned* by him to be his instruments in a world that so desperately needs the Saviour. Are we up for the challenge?

What Will we Ask for Today?

'So give your servant a discerning heart to govern your people and to distinguish between right and wrong. For who is able to govern this great people of yours?' (v 9).

Following the death of King David, Solomon's throne is firmly established. The Lord appears to Solomon in a dream, saying:

'Ask for whatever you want me to give you' (v 5).

Let's stop here and think for a moment. If God were to come to *us* in a similar kind of dream, what would we ask for? Some might ask for money; a job; a better place to live; more security. Others might ask for a child; good health; a long life; more friends. But would many ask for a discerning heart? For wisdom?

'Ah, but I'm not a king or queen,' we might say. Yet I'm sure people come to you, as they do to me, for advice; to discuss their problems, asking what we would do if it were us in their position. If we were blessed with godly wisdom and discernment, we would know how best to respond. We'd be better equipped to point them in the right direction. And we would also be better off making our *own* decisions and making the right choices in life.

Because Solomon asked for what was needed to rule the people of God, he was blessed further: riches, honour, a long life (vv 13-14). In response to all of this, the new king worshipped God:

He returned to Jerusalem, stood before the ark of the Lord's covenant and sacrificed burnt offerings and fellowship offerings (v 15).

As we bow in prayer before God right now, what will we ask him for today? There's nothing wrong with asking for good health or food to eat; for friends or even for a child. But first and foremost, let's ask him for a humble heart that is totally devoted to the Lord, so we can be all he wants us to be – for him, and for others.

Preparation

'Prepare the way for the Lord; make His paths straight!' (v 3 HCSB).

The Gospel of Mark can be thought of as a beautiful orchestral piece. Its melody: the interweaving of healing, preaching and parables. Its counter-melody: that of passion, crucifixion, death and resurrection. Its tempo: fast-moving, with pithy statements and short paragraphs. Its texture: soothing, as it emphasises the strong, yet gentle, credentials of Jesus – Servant and Son of God.

Right at the start Mark introduces John the Baptist, who makes preparation for the presentation of Jesus to the world:

'Someone more powerful than I will come after me. I am not worthy to stoop down and untie the strap of His sandals' (v 7 HCSB).

John the Baptist, although a powerful preacher and one who had many followers himself, played 'second fiddle' – to use a term as we think of this orchestral work that Mark presents to us. This was John's given mission, his ministry; to prepare the way for the Messiah. He told Israel to repent, to prepare herself for the Kingdom of God. And he was comfortable in his mission, remaining faithful to it – to the point of imprisonment and ultimate death.

How are *we* preparing others for a personal encounter with Jesus? It is also *our* mission to point others to the 'first chair' player – Christ himself. Then, as we move forward in following him daily, we encourage others to do likewise:

… they left their father Zebedee in the boat with the hired men and followed Him (v 20 HCSB).

Prayer
Father, as we read through this fascinating and gripping Gospel, prepare our hearts to receive from you each day. Then help us in the preparation of leading *others* into the presence of Jesus.

The Lowered Mat

… they made an opening in the roof above Jesus and, after digging through it, lowered the mat the paralysed man was lying on. When Jesus saw their faith, he said to the paralytic, 'Son, your sins are forgiven' (vv 4-5).

Mark leads us straight into the ministry of Jesus. He takes us to Capernaum, to a home where many people have gathered to hear Jesus speak. The house is filled to capacity. Even outside, people are trying to get a glimpse of Jesus and hear what he has to say.

Four men arrive – carrying their paralytic friend on a mat. But they cannot get near Jesus. Somehow, they manage to get on the roof. They claw out an opening, lower the mat in front of Jesus – then believe a miracle will take place.

It's good to have friends! What would we ever do without them? People we can call when in need of a listening ear. But it's also important to *be* a friend to others. To take the initiative. This is what the four men did as they brought their friend to Jesus.

So, who do we identify with in this story?

Jesus? It's not presumptuous to say this. Often we see people suffering – physically, emotionally, spiritually. God's Spirit can work through us, for we are Christ's hands and feet.

The friends? When we see a need, most of us will support as best we can. We desire to be a friend to others – by listening, encouraging; bringing a sense of hope to people around us.

The paralytic? Sometimes we simply feel helpless – broken. We are in need of healing. If we want to move forward, we need to be restored. We desperately need the touch of Jesus on our lives.

The teachers of the law? Do we ever doubt, becoming sceptical?

The crowd? They witnessed a miracle that day, seeing the man stand, take his mat and walk – his sins forgiven. Their response:

This amazed everyone and they praised God, saying, 'We have never seen anything like this!' (v 12).

PRAYER
Lord, thank you for healing and forgiving me!

Caring for People in Need

You insult your Maker when you exploit the powerless; when you're kind to the poor, you honor God (v 31 MSG).

In December 2014, General André Cox had the privilege of visiting the Vatican, to hold the first-ever private meeting between a Pope and a Salvation Army General. They had conversation and prayer together, speaking of how The Salvation Army and the Roman Catholic Church are united in a desire to share the love of God with others. To especially care for people in need.

I am not rich, compared with many wealthy people. But I *am* rich when I think of the world at large. Probably you find yourself in a similar situation. So how can we care *well*? How do we choose where and to whom we should share any resources we might possess? Today's reading tells us:

It's criminal to ignore a neighbor in need (v 21 MSG).

And is it really just about money? Giving financially to help the poor is important, no question. But being a *friend* is perhaps of even more importance. It's about caring for others by giving them respect, a sense of dignity, and including others, so they become part of *us*. We can help lessen the gap between rich and poor by walking with those who have so little materially; also being available for those who have emotional or spiritual needs. When we are 'kind to the poor', when we are a friend to a neighbour in need, we 'honour God'. And isn't that what life as a Christian is all about?

The General and the Pope met to join their hearts in praying for the world. Let us do likewise – praying for our neighbours living next door as well as those on the other side of the globe. This will bless us, bless them, and it will honour our Maker.

PRAYER
Lord God, help me to pray daily for those people who are in need. And help me see how I can be of help in practical ways, to alleviate their poverty.

They Shall Come

'People will come from east and west and north and south, and will take their places at the feast in the kingdom of God' (v 29).

Our song for today by the late General John Gowans, and set to music by Retired General John Larsson, comes from the musical *The Blood of the Lamb* – premiered in public at The Salvation Army's 1978 International Congress in London:

> They shall come from the east, they shall come from the west,
> And sit down in the Kingdom of God;
> Both the rich and the poor, the despised, the distressed,
> They'll sit down in the Kingdom of God.
> And none will ask what they have been
> Provided that their robes are clean;
> They shall come from the east, they shall come from the west,
> And sit down in the Kingdom of God.
>
> (*SASB* 1011 v 1)

Close your eyes for a moment. Picture people – of all ages, nationalities and economic status – coming together with faces aglow, ready to take their place in God's Kingdom. *All* who love God, invited. *All* who call on his name as Saviour and Lord, accepted. *Welcomed. Blessed.* Can you visualise it? What a sight!

As we join our hearts in singing this final verse may we know, no matter what we are facing, that all will be *well* when one day we embrace one another and sit down, with God, in his Kingdom!

> They shall come from the east, they shall come from the west,
> And sit down in the Kingdom of God;
> Out of great tribulation to triumph and rest
> They'll sit down in the Kingdom of God.
> From every tribe and every race,
> All men as brothers shall embrace;
> They shall come from the east, they shall come from the west,
> And sit down in the Kingdom of God.

Blessings of the Holy Spirit

Guest writer Major Florence Pamacheche from Zimbabwe provides our Pentecost series

Just imagine. What in the world would you do for God all by yourself and in your own power? Nothing! God created us in his image and after his likeness so that it would be possible for us to be filled with his Spirit.

The Holy Spirit is one of the greatest gifts that a Christian could ever have. This truth is even more profound when we recognise that whatever we do for the Lord is worthless unless it is done through the Holy Spirit. Nothing we do for God really matters until we take full advantage of the Holy Spirit in our lives.

Our service to God becomes acceptable to him when it is rendered through the Holy Spirit. Therefore we must learn to always honour the Holy Spirit and appreciate his presence in our lives. His presence is the most important thing to us.

Remember, life is nothing without the Holy Spirit. When we get to know him and have fellowship with him, our lives take on a new meaning.

Please join me in a journey to discover how the Holy Spirit transforms, recreates, empowers and blesses our Christian life so as to become Christlike, confident and compassionate in our ministry.

Major Florence Pamacheche and her husband served as Salvation Army officers in corps (church), school administration posts, and then at Territorial Headquarters in Harare. After she was widowed she held appointments at the Army's officer training colleges in Zimbabwe and Liberia. At the time of writing she is Territorial Education Secretary, Zimbabwe.

The major holds a Bachelor of Science in Counselling and a Diploma in Education.

The Holy Spirit Brings us Hope

'For nothing is impossible with God' (v 37).

The Holy Spirit is the third person of the Trinity. He lives and works in Christians. He came at Pentecost in a powerful way. He is known for his omniscience (1 Corinthians 2:10-12), omnipresence (Psalm 139:7-12) and omnipotence (Luke 1:35).

Verse 35 in the opening chapter of Luke's Gospel is a direct declaration of Jesus' divine conception. The association of the Holy Spirit with power is frequently mentioned by Luke (Luke 1:17; 4:14; Acts 1:8; 6:6-8; 10:38). Nothing will be impossible. Regardless of how circumstances may seem, God keeps his promise. What he says he will do, he will fulfil. The Holy Spirit brings hope to the heart of every Christian.

What is hope? Hope is not what you expect, it is what you would never dream of. It is a wild, improbable tale with a 'pinch-me, I'm dreaming' ending. It is Abraham adjusting his bifocals, so to speak, so he can see not his grandson, but his son (Genesis 21:1-5). It is Zechariah left speechless by the thought of his wife Elizabeth, grey-haired and pregnant (Luke 1:18-20).

Hope is not a wish granted or a favour performed. No, it is far greater than that. It is an unpredictable dependence on God the Holy Spirit who loves to surprise us out of our socks.

PONDER
What are your dreams? Ask the Holy Spirit to show you what he would love you to do, and then ask him for the power to do it.

The Holy Spirit is our Joy

For the kingdom of God is … righteousness, peace and joy in the Holy Spirit (Romans 14:17).

It is natural to be joyful when everything around you is working out alright. But at times we face trials and tribulations and the joy disappears. In January 2011, I boarded a plane for the first time when I left Zimbabwe on a mission to serve Christ in Monrovia, Liberia. After the passengers had boarded the plane the crew introduced themselves to us and our stopovers were outlined as Nairobi in Kenya and Accra, Ghana. As we cruised at 30,000 feet in the sky towards Accra, serious turbulence occurred. Our plane was shaking and we were told to fasten our seat belts.

The captain announced, 'Ladies and gentlemen, we are supposed to land in Accra but we cannot. We have to choose an alternative airport.' The cabin became quiet and I am sure everyone went into prayer. After about 20 minutes the captain broke the silence: 'Ladies and gentlemen, we *are* now landing in Accra.' When we touched down, there was a round of applause from the passengers and a united 'Thank you, Jesus.'

It was then I was reminded that on the Christian journey we are promised a safe landing in Heaven by our Captain, Jesus Christ – but not a turbulent-free trip. However, the Holy Spirit is always there to keep us safe in the turbulence of life. So we should be joyful all the time, knowing that we are never alone.

We must not sorrow, 'for the joy of the LORD is your strength' (Nehemiah 8:10) and 'Those who sow in tears shall reap in joy' (Psalm 126:5 *NKJV*).

PRAYER
Holy Spirit, help me to partake of your joy when I'm experiencing life's turbulences.

The Holy Spirit is the Intercessor

… the Spirit helps us in our weakness. We do not know what to pray for, but the Spirit himself intercedes for us with groans that words cannot express … because the Spirit intercedes for the saints in accordance with God's will (vv 26-27).

How comforting it is to know that the Holy Spirit bears us up in our hour of need, when we do not know what to pray for as we ought. He intercedes: 'the Spirit prays for us in ways that cannot be put into words' (v 26 *CEV*).

The Christian's possession of the Holy Spirit is not only evidence of their present salvation, but also a pledge of their future inheritance. We are saved by faith, but hope accompanies salvation. As hope sustains Christians when they suffer, in the same way the Holy Spirit helps them when they pray. We may not know what to pray for or how best to pray; but just as when we suffer we groan and mourn, so when we pray it is the Holy Spirit who, on our behalf, groans in unspoken words that cannot be expressed in human language.

In the year of our Lord 2007, I lost my husband to Hodgkin lymphoma. It all happened so quickly, as in a fast-action movie. I lost concentration on whatever I wanted to do, be it prayer, reading, my devotions. I would close my eyes, say a word or two, then find myself back to the thought of my loss.

One night I woke up and tried to pray. I knelt and found myself with no words to say – only tears. It was at that time God sent me a Christian friend, a daughter in Christ, who would visit me regularly. Each time she came we talked, cried and prayed together. The heaviness on my heart gradually disappeared.

I had come to terms with the fact that I could not change what had happened, and I am certain the Holy Spirit was interceding for me.

PRAYER
Mighty Spirit, dwell with me; I myself would mighty be,
Mighty so as to prevail Where unaided man must fail;
Ever by a mighty hope Pressing on and bearing up.
**   (Thomas Lynch, *SASB* 300 v 4)**

Always Praising the Lord

Then they worshipped him and returned to Jerusalem with great joy.
And they stayed continually at the temple, praising God (vv 52-53).

As the disciples returned from the Mount of Olives to Jerusalem, people might have looked at them expecting to see on their faces expressions of sorrow, confusion and defeat. Instead they saw gladness and triumph. The disciples did not mourn over lost hopes. They had seen their risen Saviour, and the words of his parting promise rang constantly in their ears: 'I am going to send you what my Father has promised; but stay in the city until you have been clothed with power from on high' (v 49).

In obedience they waited in Jerusalem for the promise of the Father, the outpouring of the Holy Spirit. They did not wait in idleness. They were continually in the temple praising and blessing God. They also met together to present their requests to the Father in the name of Jesus.

They knew they had a representation in Heaven, an advocate at the throne of God. As they bowed daily to God they were repeating the assurance from Christ: 'Whatever you ask the Father in My name He will give you. Until now you have asked nothing in My name. Ask, and you will receive, that your joy may be full' (John 16:23-24 *NKJV*).

In 2 Chronicles 20:20-23 we read how the Israelite army, led by King Jehoshaphat, sang praises to the Lord before facing enemy forces. As they did, they declared that the battle was not theirs but the Lord's and God could accomplish his purpose *without* an earthly army. They celebrated victory even *before* the battle – and God honoured their faith amid difficulties.

PONDER
Today, ask God to give you praise in your heart and on your lips each time you face trials. Be an overcomer!

Unity of Purpose

May the God who gives endurance and encouragement give you a spirit of unity among yourselves as you follow Christ Jesus (Romans 15:5).

In the upper room the disciples had gathered for a special purpose: to wait for the promised gift of the Holy Spirit from the Father. They would set aside personal feelings and commit themselves to one task – witnessing about the Lord Jesus Christ.

They prayed with intense earnestness for the ability to engage with people and speak words that would lead sinners to Christ. They came close together in Christian fellowship. As they drew nearer to God, they realised what a privilege had been theirs to be associated so closely with Christ.

Perhaps sadness filled their hearts as they thought of how many times they had grieved Jesus by their slowness of understanding, their failure to comprehend the lessons that, for their good, he was trying to teach them. Now they must put away all differences of opinion, any desire for power, and be united in purpose.

As we remember this unique gathering of the disciples, let us earnestly come together in prayer and seek a renewing of our hearts and minds. Think how, at your place of worship, in your workplace or maybe among your family, you might need to discard any differences you have. Then, united in prayer, move forward to accomplish your spiritual goals.

> Blest be the tie that binds
> Our hearts in Christian love;
> The fellowship of kindred minds
> Is like to that above.
>
> Before our Father's throne
> We pour our ardent prayers;
> Our fears, our hopes, our aims are one,
> Our comforts and our cares.
>   (John Fawcett, *SASB* 812 vv 1-2)

Searching all Hearts

As for you, my son Solomon, know the God of your father, and serve Him with a loyal heart and with a willing mind; for the LORD searches all hearts and understands all the intent of the thoughts. If you seek Him, He will be found by you (v 9 NKJV).

As the disciples waited for the promised Holy Spirit they spent 40 days in earnest prayer. These days of preparation were times of heart searching. The disciples felt their spiritual need and they cried to the Lord for the holy anointing of the Spirit that was to fit them for their work of soul saving.

They did not ask for blessings for themselves only; they were filled also with the burden of salvation of souls. And they claimed the power that Christ had promised.

True service for God is more than intellect and reasoning. It requires a commitment of our emotions as well. This was precisely where Solomon failed. Even though he had great wisdom (2 Chronicles 1:12; 9:3, 22-23), he allowed his heart to turn aside from God because he loved foreign women (1 Kings 11:1-4). Loyalty of heart is essential for faithful, effective service. This is why King David asked God to examine his thoughts, to cleanse him of sin, so that he might enter into everlasting life (Psalm 139:23-24).

Verse 5 of Song 623 in *The Song Book of The Salvation Army* has been my prayer in life:

> Take my will and make it thine,
> It shall be no longer mine;
> Take my heart, it is thine own,
> It shall be thy royal throne.
> (Frances Ridley Havergal)

Can it be your prayer, too?

Change is Needed!

All of them were filled with the Holy Spirit and began to speak in other tongues as the Spirit enabled them (v 4).

A sound like a rushing, mighty wind was needed to attract the multitudes to the small gathering of apostles. The Holy Spirit came upon the waiting, praying disciples with an awesomeness that reached every heart.

The Spirit gave them the ability to speak in languages they had not previously known. Everyone heard them speak in their own language. It was a sign from Heaven – a supernatural event. The disciples had been transformed. They had been empowered for ministry.

God's Spirit does not impart fear or cowardice. He gives us power and love (2 Timothy 1:7). We have the good sense to reject sin and to serve God fearlessly.

There had been a great change in the disciples' lives. But to change is not easy. Most of us develop comfort zones, where we rest and perhaps, in time, forget Pentecost. Oh how we need another Pentecost today! Do we want the same empowering the disciples experienced when they received the Holy Spirit?

'Spirit of the living God, fall afresh on me' (*SASB* 312). This is my daily prayer – for the Holy Spirit to work renewal in *my* heart.

PONDER

What comfort zones are you in? Where is change needed in your life today?

An Agent of Change

'"I am sending you to them to open their eyes and turn them from darkness to light, and from the power of Satan to God, so that they may receive forgiveness of sins and a place among those who are sanctified by faith in me"' (vv 17-18).

The true Christian is a symbol of change wherever they are. It is impossible for a room to remain dark when a light bulb has been switched on. The Christian is an agent of change in our dark world – through the power of the Holy Spirit. It is what the Word of God declares: 'You will receive power when the Holy Spirit comes on you; and you will be my witnesses in Jerusalem, and in all Judea and Samaria, and to the ends of the earth' (Acts 1:8).

'Power' is the dynamic ability to cause change. The Holy Spirit gives every Christian the power to effect lasting change – in the family, community, workplace, church and the nation. God has entrusted the life-changing gospel of Jesus Christ to all Christians.

In Matthew 5:13-14 Jesus tells us that we are the salt of the earth and the light of the world. Salt preserves, heals, gives taste and prevents decay; light gives people vision and direction. We cannot simply sit back, fold our arms and let the devil rampage. We must place him where he belongs – under our feet!

Jesus also commands: 'Go and make disciples of all nations, baptising them in the name of the Father and of the Son and of the Holy Spirit' (Matthew 28:19). Only the gospel of Jesus Christ can bring true satisfaction to the world.

You are God's minister of reconciliation to spread the good news and turn hearts of men and women from darkness to light.

PRAYER
Father God, thank you for making me your agent of change by the empowering of the Holy Spirit.

The Holy Spirit Convicts of Sin

'When he comes, he will convict the world of guilt in regard to sin and righteousness and judgment' (v 8).

I magine what the world would be if the Holy Spirit was not there to convict us of our sin. Everybody would be living in an 'I am always right and I know it all' world. This would bring calamity – to families, communities, workplaces and the world at large. It would indicate a great disobedience to the Spirit, who is there to convict us of sin and make sure we obey God by turning away from sin and living a holy life.

We read in 1 Samuel chapter 15 how King Saul was instructed by the Holy Spirit, through Samuel the prophet, that Israel should not spare anything of the Amalekites but destroy everything, including their livestock. Saul and the people kept alive Agag, the king of Amalek, and the best livestock they found in the land.

Saul thought he had a sensible reason for disobeying the prophet's instruction: he said he had kept the best livestock because the people wanted to offer them as a sacrifice to God. But Saul's responsibility was to make sure the people obeyed God. He failed to do this. As a consequence of his disobedience to the Holy Spirit, Saul lost the throne of Israel and the kingdom was removed from his lineage.

Without the Spirit's convicting work, people can never see themselves as sinners. The Holy Spirit also convicts unbelievers through those believers who witness about Christ.

Prayer
I thank you, Father, for calling me to be obedient to the Holy Spirit. I ask you to remove from my heart any pride, stubbornness and rebellion.

The Holy Spirit Indwells and Changes Lives

*But if Christ is in you … your spirit is alive because of righteousness
(Romans 8:10).*

Paul's benediction to the Christians in Corinth invokes the blessing of the triune God: grace from the Lord Jesus Christ, the love of God, and the fellowship of the Holy Spirit (2 Corinthians 13:14). Here Paul identifies the solution to many of the Corinthians' problems. If the Holy Spirit dwells within them, the Spirit empowers them to live righteously.

Instead of fighting each other, with bouts of 'quarrelling, jealousy, outbursts of anger' (12:20), they could love and encourage each other. The Spirit would reconcile them to each other. They needed grace, not selfishness; love, not anger; communion, not conflict – all coming from God through his Holy Spirit. We need these blessings, too, as Christians today. The late General John Gowans echoed Paul's sentiments in his prayerful song, 'How much more':

> If men will often share their gladness,
> If men respond when children cry,
> If men can feel each other's sadness,
> Each other's tears attempt to dry,
>> Then how much more shall God our Father
>> In love forgive, in love forgive!
>> Then how much more shall God our Father
>> Our wants supply, and none deny!
>>   (*SASB* 467 v 3)

We need to show God's love in forgiveness. We need to improve our relations within our communities, displaying spiritual maturity by God's grace. With the indwelling of the Holy Spirit, we can be empowered to live in ways that bless others and God.

PONDER
Should you pray for the Holy Spirit to fill you and empower you for service? Are you also praying for someone to receive salvation by God's grace today?

The Holy Spirit Sanctifies

And Joshua said to the people, 'Sanctify yourselves, for tomorrow the LORD will do wonders among you' (v 5 NKJV).

As God guided the Israelites into the Promised Land, he instructed them to purify themselves before crossing the Jordan River. God stopped the Jordan River in flood stage so that people crossed easily into Canaan. The Ark of the Covenant and the priests led this procession. The miracle had come after the sanctification.

To sanctify is to set apart as holy, to consecrate to religious use, to make holy. In the Book of Joshua we find the word sanctify means to separate from things that are not clean, common. It is God's command that Christians should be holy, set apart for special service in his ministry (1 Peter 1:14-16).

I have seen farmers prepare seed for planting. They select some particular seed to plant in a field with rich soil and under special conditions. The seed had been stored in a separate storeroom so that it did not get mixed with the grain that will be consumed by the household. The next season there was seed available – set apart – for planting.

God has set aside Christians because he wants to make use of them in his ministry. He wants to do great things among his followers. William Pearson's song reminds us:

> I'm set apart for Jesus
> To be a king and priest …
> My all is consecrated
> Unto the living God.
>   (*SASB* 255 v 1)

Sanctification cleans the heart, makes our hearts God's altar, drives our foes away, gives strength for trials and is a shield when darts are hurled. Oh what a wonderful God we serve!

PONDER
What steps are you taking to fulfil God's will? Are you following his instruction for sanctification so that he will do great things in your life?

The Holy Spirit Helps in our Struggles

… who comforts us in all our tribulation, that we may be able to comfort those who are in any trouble, with the comfort with which we ourselves are comforted by God (v 4 NKJV).

Something happens to us when we struggle with problems – whether they are physical, emotional, financial or spiritual. We can become victims and be paralysed by our problems, or are victors by allowing God to help us grow through these difficulties.

Young David is an example of a man of God who trusted in the Holy Spirit (see 1 Samuel chapter 17). He was a winner who had faced, fought and finished off his giants in life. He never allowed struggles to be detours that would drain or derail his faith.

Struggling with life's difficulties makes us stronger, a little more capable, enabling us to comfort others who experience their own pain. We need to remain faithful to God and always trust in his never-failing hand. God the Holy Spirit is the mighty warrior who is great in battle. With him we will not lose (as promised in Isaiah 49:13 and John 14:16).

Jesus knows all about our struggles. Any difficulties we face in life are short-lived. A divine inheritance shall be our reward for faithfulness to God. Renewing that faithfulness should be our priority when beginning every new day.

We are responsible to the will of God for our victories, but we are dependent upon the Holy Spirit for the power to overcome our struggles.

Prayer

Holy Spirit, help us not to minimise our struggles and help us to recognise that any struggle we have is small in comparison to the great God we serve.

The Fruit of the Spirit

But the fruit of the Spirit is love, joy, peace, patience, kindness, goodness, faithfulness, gentleness and self-control. Against such things there is no law (vv 22-23).

Paul is encouraging the Christians to walk in the Spirit, that is, to obey the prompting of the Spirit so as not to give in to the lust of the flesh. Paul reinforces the work of the Holy Spirit by further instructing the Galatians to bear fruit that show they are walking in the Spirit of God.

A Christian who walks in the Spirit will not provoke others or envy others. The way we live, the things we say, the attitudes we entertain, the lifestyle we adopt are all continuously producing either positive or negative results in society.

We live in an atmosphere of antagonism, an environment of enmity. Yet amid all this, Christ calls us to produce peace. This peace is an inner attitude of tranquillity and tolerance in the face of angry attacks. It is a willingness to accept the assaults of others even at the price of personal humiliation.

This means that even if I know my enemies, I am still at peace with them. I will continue to be joyful in trials and tribulations, and I will be patient with God and in my relationships because I know that 'joy *comes* in the morning' (Psalm 30:5 *NKJV*).

PONDER
How do you exhibit your faith? Do you show gentleness and self-control?

The Holy Spirit Gives Discernment

We have not received the spirit of the world but the Spirit who is from God, that we may understand what God has freely given us (v 12).

It is common to hear people say, 'The majority cannot be wrong'. These words cannot be true, and there is no Scripture that supports them. The Word of God records how the whole world was destroyed and only a family of eight – Noah and his household – was saved. The reason was that Noah lived a life that was in accordance with God's will and purpose. Doesn't this support the fact that the statement about 'the majority' *is* wrong?

Christians should learn to follow the Holy Spirit and not the voice of people. Learning to discern the voice of the Spirit from people's opinions is very important when Christians have to make judgements and decisions. God does not go by numbers; he does not speak to favour the majority. He speaks according to what is written in his Word, through the Holy Spirit.

Every Christian should follow the Spirit of God in the direction he has given for their life: 'When he, the Spirit of truth, comes, he will guide you into all truth' (John 16:13). He is the greatest friend and best teacher who guides us and makes God's presence tangible to us.

We should yield to the Holy Spirit through the Word of God and do what it tells us to do. We will find ourselves making the best decisions and the right choices the first time, be at the right place at the right time, and live a life worthy of emulation.

PRAYER
Thank you, Jesus, for the Holy Spirit. I yield my spirit to him to be instructed, directed and led in all my dealings.

(We thank Major Pamacheche for her witness and ministry of blessing through this series of devotions. – B.I.)

Building up the Temple

In the four hundred and eightieth year after the Israelites had come out of Egypt … he began to build the temple of the LORD (6:1).

Solomon asked God for 'a discerning heart' (1 Kings 3:9) in order to rule his people. God granted him his desire, giving to Solomon both wisdom and great insight. This gave the king fame, for he became 'wiser than any other man' (4:31). Because of this, King Solomon wrote many proverbs and songs: 'He spoke three thousand proverbs and his songs numbered a thousand and five' (4:32).

Solomon was also the perfect person to build the Temple in Jerusalem. There was 'rest on every side' (5:4), because David had previously fought battle after battle – in order that there be peace in the land. The timing was right. David had paved the way by establishing good relationships and also finding people who would contribute to the building project.

It all had to be perfect: the walls; the windows; the different floors; the stairways; the roofing; the wood to be used; the gold; the cherubs; the altar; the inner sanctuary. The Temple took seven years to build (6:38) but it was finally ready. And it was magnificent!

Only the very best is required for God, for he is to be honoured and worshipped. Do *we* present to him only our very best? Our place of worship may not be fancy to look at but it should be sparkling clean! It may not be adorned with gold, but our corps or church building should *shine* for the Lord. The people who gather to worship may not be perfect, but we should all approach God with a sense of awe and reverence – for we gather together to worship the King of kings!

As we bow to worship him, in the quietness of our home or office or some sacred place, may we realise we are *all* part of building up the temple of the Lord. We are his workmanship, co-workers with Christ – reaching out to others, all for the extension of God's Kingdom.

PRAYER
Help me, Lord, in the building up of *your* temple by sharing your love with at least one person today.

Dedication and Benediction

Then Solomon … spread out his hands towards heaven and said:
'O Lord, God of Israel, there is no God like you in heaven above or
on earth below' (vv 22-23).

Once the Temple was built, the Ark of the Covenant was placed in the Most Holy Place – beneath the wings of the cherubim – representing the very presence of God. Solomon then blessed all those gathered and prayed a prayer of dedication.

Solomon pours out his heart to God in worship, with hands held high and knees bent in true humility. The king acknowledges that the Lord cannot be contained by the Temple he has built, yet is confident God answers prayers in keeping with his covenant:

' … you who keep your covenant of love with your servants who continue
wholeheartedly in your way' (v 23).

Are *we* confident God hears and answers our prayers – as long as they are consistent with his promises? We look at the world situation: wars, conflict, injustice, suffering, exploitation, poverty. Do we believe God loves and cares for his people? Do we believe *we* can make a difference in making the world a better place for us all?

We close with a Franciscan benediction. As we read it together, may we dedicate ourselves afresh to God's work, and his mission:

May God bless you with discomfort at half-truths and superficial relationships, so that you may live deep within your heart.

May God bless you with anger at injustice, oppression and exploitation, so that you may work for justice, freedom and peace.

May God bless you with tears to shed for those who suffer pain, rejection and hunger so that you may reach out your hand to comfort them and to turn their pain into joy.

And may God bless you with enough foolishness to believe that you can make a difference, so that you can do what others claim cannot be done to bring justice and kindness to all people. Amen.

Compromise

'As for you, if you walk before me in integrity of heart and uprightness ... I will establish your royal throne over Israel for ever ... But if you or your sons turn away from me ... I will cut off Israel from the land I have given them and will reject this temple I have consecrated for my Name' (9:4-7).

King Solomon was at the top of his game. He had built the Temple, and all was well. But God gave him a warning. If the king followed in the footsteps of his father, David, the Lord would prosper and bless him. But if Solomon strayed from God's path, he would be severely disciplined, along with his people.

Solomon's fame and fortune got the best of him. He began to make drastic compromises, beginning by accumulating *many* wives:

King Solomon, however, loved many foreign women ... He had seven hundred wives of royal birth and three hundred concubines, and his wives led him astray (11:1, 3).

That's a lot of women for one man! Earthly pursuits, paganism, lust – all turned the king's heart away from God. In fact, Scripture tells us Solomon 'did evil in the eyes of the LORD' (v 6), compromising God's holy standards. And what was God's response?

'Since this is your attitude and you have not kept my covenant and my decrees, which I commanded you, I will most certainly tear the kingdom away from you' (v 11).

When we veer off the path God has for us, he is not pleased – at all! *Is* there something not good in our lives? Only we can answer this. Then we must make a decision: will we make things *right*?

PRAYER
Cleanse my heart, O God. May I never compromise your holy standards for my life.

Remedy for Rejection

Then Jesus told them, 'A prophet is honoured everywhere except in his own hometown and among his relatives and his own family' (v 4 NLT).

Rejection is tough. To be rejected by a certain community is never easy. To be rejected by another person is hard going. But to be rejected by family and close friends is tragic and painful. The emotions run so deep. But it happens, sadly, all the time. How do we cope? How can we get through such terrible times and move forward with any sense of dignity?

We can easily feel worthless when rejected; feel that we no longer have value. Yes, people can come alongside us, saying everything will work out eventually. But rejection hurts, there is no doubt about it. And we have all been there, in one form or another.

Jesus also experienced rejection – in his home town. So much so that he could not perform any miracles there. He was so 'amazed at their unbelief' (v 6 *NLT*).

So, how *do* we deal with rejection? What's the remedy? The Scripture passage tells of the disciples moving out, engaged in mission. Even there, it could be that there is rejection:

'But if any place refuses to welcome you or listen to you, shake its dust from your feet as you leave' (v 11 NLT).

We are never to give up! Rather, to keep going – for God's sake:

So the disciples went out, telling everyone they met to repent of their sins and turn to God (v 12 NLT).

English writer and theologian G.K. Chesterton once said: 'When it rains on your parade, look up rather than down. Without the rain, there would be no rainbow.' It is so easy to get caught up in sadness, depression, self-pity – all because of rejection. We need to ask God to help us see the remedy – fixing our eyes on the mission he has for each one of us. Are we looking up? *Do* we see the rainbow?

True Worship

'Why don't your disciples live according to the tradition of the elders instead of eating their food with "unclean" hands?' (v 5).

We can so easily get caught up in rituals. Doing things simply out of duty. Attending church because we are supposed to do so. Saying grace before a meal out of mere habit. Singing spiritual songs or hymns without thinking about the words or implication.

The Pharisees and teachers of the law consistently wanted to trip up Jesus in what he or his disciples were doing or preaching. Today's Scripture passage concerns the ritual of rinsing hands before eating. Yet nothing in the Old Testament requires this of lay people – only priests.

Jesus responds to their accusations by saying true worship is not about following rituals or rules; it's all about what is going on *in our heart*. This is what really matters. We are to live pure and holy lives because of an inborn desire to serve our living God. We can appear to be godly by doing all the right things; appear to be clean on the outside. But true worship is about what is going on *inside*.

What, then, is true worship all about? Possibly one of the best definitions of worship I have ever encountered is given by William Temple, a former Archbishop of Canterbury (1942-1944): 'To worship is to quicken the conscience by the holiness of God, to feed the mind with the truth of God, to purge the imagination by the beauty of God, to open the heart to the love of God, to devote the will to the purpose of God.'[2]

Will we come before Almighty God, in humble adoration – with hearts ready and willing to worship him?

PRAYER

Lord, I long to *worship* you, to commune with you, right now, in the beauty of your holiness.

Benefits and Blessings

God be merciful to us and bless us, and cause His face to shine upon us (67:1 NKJV).

Psalm 67 opens by asking God for three things: mercy, blessings, and approval. His graciousness to be poured over us; benefits and blessings given to us; his face shining upon us. When all three things take place, all is well within! For we then know we are living according to God's will for our lives.

As God shows to us his mercy, blessing us and giving us his approval, it's like rain falling upon a hill; it then runs down in streams and into the valleys. When we receive godly benefits and are blessed, we truly desire that the 'rain' filters down to bless others – and all for God's glory.

Psalm 68 continues this theme of benefits and blessings:

Blessed be the Lord, who daily loads us with benefits, The God of our salvation! (v 19 NKJV).

God daily loads us with benefits! Yet do we ever stop to think about all he *does* give us? If we are reading this, we have the gift of life itself; if someone is reading it to us, we also benefit – from the gift of a family member or a good friend. We have the benefits of health, home, food, safety. We have the blessings of family, friends, church, community.

I recently received a beautiful bouquet of flowers from some family members, and was deeply touched! The colours were vibrant; the fragrance permeated our home. It brightened my day greatly, and many days that followed. It was a reminder that God *loads* us with benefits that encourage, uplift, strengthen and *bless* us, daily.

Action
Let's choose to bless at least one person today by doing something special for them. A loving smile is a start! Whatever 'benefit' we choose, it will bring joy to their heart – and will also bless the Lord!

Give us a Day of Wonders

'Stop and consider God's wonders' (37:14).

Do you ever long for a day of wonders? Time just to think and ponder on everything God has created and made for us; to meditate on all he has done and is still doing for us?

> Give us a day of wonders, Jehovah, bare thine arm;
> Pour out thy Holy Spirit, Make known thy healing balm;
> Give blessings without number, Supply us from thy store;
> Dear Saviour, richly bless us, Baptise us more and more.
> (*SASB* 334 v 1).

This song for today was written in the late 19th century by Colonel John Lawley while on board a train travelling to the opening of a new Salvation Army corps (church). Wonderful! Yet God wants *us*, the worshippers, to also be blessed and filled with his Holy Spirit:

> We offer thee this temple, With power, Lord, enter in
> And teach us when we worship Or wage the war with sin.
> O may the sinner find thee Within these hallowed walls,
> Here may young, eager spirits Obey when Jesus calls!
> (v 2)

Satan would love to destroy us. There's so much in the world that can tempt and lure us, causing us to stumble. We plead to the Lord for protection. We pray, day in and day out, that God will be with us, will bless us, as we strive to live for him. Let's join our voices as we sing this final verse and refrain – expecting God to open our eyes and give us, truly, a day of wonder!

> Give courage for the battle, Give strength thy foes to slay;
> Give light to cheer the darkness, Give grace from day-to-day;
> Give rest amidst life's conflict, Give peace when lions roar;
> Give faith to fight with patience Till fighting days are o'er.
>   Lord, hear us while we pray! Lord, hear us while we pray!
>   Now thy Spirit give, let the dying live, And bless us here today.

Influence

'My father made your yoke heavy; I will make it even heavier. My father scourged you with whips; I will scourge you with scorpions' (v 14).

When Solomon died, his son Rehoboam became king. But unlike his wise father, and definitely unlike his grandfather David – who was a man after God's own heart (1 Samuel 13:14) – Rehoboam wanted to prove he was his own man, powerful in his own right.

Solomon was *not* wise in many things – such as making labour very difficult for his people. But the new king was far worse. So some of the Israel assembly came to him, begging that things become easier for the people, and their heavy yoke be lightened. They pledged their allegiance if this took place.

Rehoboam sought out the elders who had faithfully served his father, asking for their advice. He also consulted his friends on the matter. He liked what his pals told him – thinking their conclusions would prove him far more in control. But it all backfired, resulting in complete rebellion:

So Israel has been in rebellion against the house of David to this day (v 19).

Who is it we go to for advice? Who *influences* us the most – and is this a good thing? For all of us, on a regular basis, need to seek out godly people to guide us, to steer us in the right direction, to help us make good choices. Are we influenced by Spirit-filled people, keeping us on the right path? Then what about us? Do we try to influence others by taking time with them; praying for them; seeking God's wisdom for their lives?

Rehoboam wanted to prove himself and, in so doing, things went downhill fast – for him, and for Israel as a united kingdom. May we never get off track, away from God's direction for our lives. Rather, may we daily be open to the good and godly influence of others. And then, in turn, let's try to influence *others* – by the way we live, and as we point them to our loving Saviour.

Civil War

There was war between Rehoboam and Jeroboam (15:6).

The Lord chose David and his descendants to rule his people. His first descendant, Solomon, started off well – asking God for discernment. But his wealth and pride soon got the better of him, resulting in him making poor choices. Solomon's son, Rehoboam, was power-hungry and arrogant, neglecting to seek God for direction. Because of this, there was rebellion – to the point of civil war.

The nation split. It was a divided kingdom. Ten tribes assembled in the north under Jeroboam's leadership; another two in the south, under King Rehoboam. God was not pleased with what happened. Seeing all the evil taking place in the north, he said to Jeroboam:

'You have done more evil than all who lived before you. You have made for yourself other gods, idols made of metal; you have provoked me to anger and thrust me behind your back' (14:9).

In the south, with Rehoboam, things were not any better:

Judah did evil in the eyes of the LORD … There were even male shrine-prostitutes … the people engaged in all the detestable practices of the nations the LORD had driven out before the Israelites (vv 22, 24).

How could things have gone so wrong? Sin! People taking things into their own hands, thinking they knew best. Forgetting God; or for certain, not calling on him to intervene. Sounds familiar? Maybe not to the extent of rejecting God completely, but perhaps *neglecting* him, failing to lean on him and commune with him.

May this never happen to us – causing war without or within.

PRAYER
God, I ask for your protection and your help – in *all* areas of my life. May I never try to take charge myself, but always rely on you alone to guide, direct and *bless* my life.

Open Heart

'As the LORD, the God of Israel, lives, whom I serve, there will be neither dew nor rain in the next few years except at my word' (v 1).

After Elijah burst onto the scene – predicting an impending drought during Ahab's reign – God told his prophet to go and hide. Elijah went to a ravine, where he was fed by ravens. When the brook dried up, the prophet was told to move on to Zarephath. There, a widow would supply him with food – even though she was poor and barely had enough for herself and her son. Yet, on his arrival, the prophet told her this wonderful news:

'The jar of flour will not be used up and the jug of oil will not run dry until the day the LORD gives rain on the land' (v 14).

A miracle! God would provide. But it did not stop there. The widow's son became very ill and died. Elijah prayed that the boy would be returned to life – and it happened. Another miracle! All because Elijah's heart was open to God. He longed to receive from God, and to impart God's marvellous grace and love to others.

Are we praying for a miracle? Do we have an open heart, wanting to receive from God? We close today with a beautiful prayer written by the late Mrs Commissioner Flora Larsson. As we pray together, may *our* hearts be open – 'as the sunflower to the sun'.

PRAYER
'Master, grant me an open heart toward you. Many times I feel that your love cannot reach me because of the barriers I myself have erected against you; barriers of unbelief, of mistrust and sometimes of sheer apathy … Master! Show me how to break them down. I want an open heart before you, a believing, responsive heart … I open my mind to the wonders of your love. Make me receptive, Lord! Let me know a fuller measure of your Spirit indwelling me. Let me live turned ever towards you as the sunflower to the sun. Grant me, Lord, an open heart, I pray.'[3]

Who Am I?

'Who do people say that I am?' (v 27 ESV).

Have you ever played the game 'Who am I?' I recall playing it as a child, mostly with my mom. She would think of someone and then I would try to guess who that someone was. If right, then it was my turn! It's important to know *who* we are; to take time for introspection. Yet some people struggle with 'self-identity' – not knowing their purpose in life.

Jesus *knew* who he was. But he was interested to know the thoughts of others. In his poem 'Bishop Blougram's Apology', Robert Browning penned these words:

> What think ye of Christ, friend? When all's done and said,
> Like you this Christianity or not?
> It may be false, but will you wish it true?
> Has it your vote to be so if it can?

Does Christianity have our vote? 'Of course!' we say. And yet, Jesus Christ: who really is he – to us? This question haunts many people – as echoed in the fundamental theme of the rock musical, *Jesus Christ Superstar*, which hit Broadway in 1971: Who really is this Jesus Christ? When Jesus posed the question to his disciples, they responded by saying some thought he was John the Baptist, Elijah, or a prophet. Jesus wanted to know *their* thoughts:

'But who do you say that I am?' (v 29 ESV).

George Bernard Shaw's play *Saint Joan* has an interesting dialogue from the 15th century between the Archbishop and Joan of Arc: 'Joan,' the Archbishop says, 'you're in love with religion.' Joan responds, 'Is there wrong in it?' 'No,' he replies, 'but there's danger in it.'

Our lives are to be centred in Jesus. For when we identify him as 'the Christ', as Peter did (v 29), we claim him to be Lord of all. It is our declaration of love and praise, but also one of obedience and sacrifice. We are willing to do *anything* for him, and at any cost. Living a life of holiness is serious business – yet what joy it brings to one's heart!

So, who are *we* – as Christians? Children, followers, servants of *Jesus*. Can there be any better self-declaration than this?

The Preservation of 'Family'

'The two will become one. So they are no longer two, but one. Let no man divide what God has put together' (vv 8-9 NLV).

In the beginning God created 'family'. He created it, I believe, for several reasons: *sociological* – integrating people, to create a sense of belonging; *psychological* – loving, then to feel we are also loved; *theological* – introducing covenant and commitment.

When we reflect upon a nuclear family, many people sense feelings of warmth, of acceptance. Yet for others, heartbreaking experiences create deep sadness. But then there is the 'family of God': believers bonded together in Christian fellowship, blessed by him.

The Creator longs for the preservation of 'family'. Yes, a nuclear family where possible – as implied by Scripture. But we must also seek after the preservation of the 'family of God'. How can we do this best?

Communication. A key word! To talk, but also to *listen* well. Sharing from the heart while keeping an open mind.

Honesty. When there is honesty and openness, relationships can grow; be nourished. We are to be trustworthy, honest people of God.

Commitment. Committed people create an atmosphere of stability, safety, security – when committed to Christ, to 'family'.

Consecration. As we consecrate ourselves to Christ, self is put to the side. We will want to give of ourselves – no matter what cost.

Love. Above all, we are to clothe ourselves with humility and love. As God so loves us, we are to love one another – from the heart.

Jesus loved, and *still* loves, all children. He said:

'Let the little children come to Me' (v 14 NLV).

That means *our* children, our *friends' and neighbours'* children, and *us* as his children – his family. How well are *we* celebrating, loving and preserving 'family'?

Mercy Drops

Save me, O God, for the waters have come up to my neck (v 1).

When I was a little girl I loved to play in the lake close to our Salvation Army camp near Toronto. One day my older sister was out deeper with her friends. I wanted to go and see her – so out I went. But my swimming skills were not that great and I began to sink. The water had 'come up to my neck' – and beyond!

I cried out to God for help, for somebody to save me. God heard my cry and sent someone just in time to save me from drowning. God had *mercy* on a little child – and I'm alive to tell the story.

David also needed to be saved. Yes, physically – for he found himself hiding in caves to escape the vengeance of a spiteful king. But he also needed to be saved from all the stress of being on the run, constantly. He needed mercy drops to fall upon him, assuring him of God's presence and protection.

We *all* need to be saved. Some in a physical sense, some emotionally. For *all* of us, we need God's mercy to fall upon us spiritually. And so, with David, we call out:

Answer me, O LORD, out of the goodness of your love; in your great mercy turn to me (v 16).

Mercy drops: to fall upon those people who are vulnerable and exploited in some way; to fall upon those who are suffering and in pain. Mercy drops, in order to be saved from all that brings destruction and devastation and distress and darkness. When we seek God in all things, our hearts will then be able to live for him:

… you who seek God, may your hearts live! (v 32).

PRAYER
O God, I love you and want to live daily for you. Save me from all that hinders – and shower me with your mercy drops, I plead!

Let the Beauty of Jesus be Seen

One thing I ask of the LORD, this is what I seek: that I may dwell in the house of the LORD all the days of my life, to gaze upon the beauty of the LORD (v 4).

This short chorus, written by the late General Albert Orsborn, makes reference to Jesus' beauty, his 'passion', his 'purity', his *loveliness*. But it primarily addresses *our* nature and how *we* are to reflect the Lord's beauty in our lives:

> Let the beauty of Jesus be seen in me,
> All his wonderful passion and purity,
> O thou Spirit divine, all my nature refine,
> Till the beauty of Jesus be seen in me.
> *(SASB* 717)

Us? Like Jesus? How can this be possible? It's true, we will never be perfect people. In fact, if you are like me, the further we travel on our spiritual journey the more we realise how *imperfect* we really are! But we *can* reflect the beauty of Jesus – asking the Holy Spirit to help us in several ways:

The words we say. Words are so important. Whether we write them in a letter or speak them to another person, they can be used to edify, encourage and bless. Our lips are to be sanctified daily by God's Spirit, so people will be aware of Christ's *beauty* in us.

The deeds we do. Sometimes we wonder what we can do to bless others. It does not have to be big. It doesn't have to take lots of time or energy. But something done for another person, in the name of Jesus, is indeed a *beautiful* thing.

The way we live. We are to ask the Holy Spirit to refine us, so we can be holy people. To embrace the fruit of the Spirit, extending love to all people. To reflect the *beauty* and holiness of Jesus, our Lord and Saviour, every day of our lives.

As we share our lives with those around us, we want the beauty of Jesus to be seen – so others will be drawn to him. If this is so for you, then please join with readers around the world to sing this refrain while we gaze on the beauty of our Lord.

God's Signature

When all the people saw this, they fell prostrate and cried, 'The LORD – he is God! The LORD – he is God!' (v 39).

After Elijah told King Ahab about the drought to come, it came – and was severe! It was God's punishment on his nation for turning their back on him. Then God wanted to create a situation to prove he was the only true God, and that only he could provide a solution for this national crisis. He again used his trusted prophet to do this, for God's signature was written over Elijah's life.

People's signatures are significant. Perhaps you own some artwork signed by the artist, or have a book signed by the author. It gives that object added meaning. Our *own* signature is important, giving weight and authentication. God wants *his* signature written upon our lives – so that no matter what we face, we know something of his power and strength, justice and mercy, grace and love.

The scene on Mount Carmel, read about in Scripture today, must have been something to behold! There were 450 prophets of Baal and 400 prophets of Asherah – against one lone believer in God Almighty. Elijah had a bull placed on the altar. The false prophets danced with fury, yelling out to Baal – for hours! – to send fire on the sacrifice:

'O Baal, answer us!' (v 26).

Can you picture it all – and can you *hear* the deafening screams and pleas to Baal? It was all in vain. Nothing happened. Then Elijah told the people to pour water over the offering and the wood – three times! He prayed, in great faith, to Almighty God for the fire to come:

Then the fire of the LORD fell and burned up the sacrifice, the wood, the stones and the soil, and also licked up the water in the trench (v 38).

Elijah's faith had God's signature of approval. Is his signature written over the tapestry and story of our lives? May it be so – for each one of us – as we experience God's power, mercy, love and grace.

A Still Small Voice

… and after the fire a still small voice (v 12 NKJV).

Many people with iPhones will be familiar with Siri – Apple's 'personal assistant'. Users can ask Siri a question and 'she' responds with the correct answer, if it's within her capability. We can speak into our iPhone, for example, and ask: 'What planes are above me right now?' Siri might respond: 'Checking my sources'; then, moments later, start listing flights, their numbers, altitudes and angles. Siri is not human. It's an inanimate object, but 'she' can utter words. A little voice – speaking through a phone.

Following the spectacular Mount Carmel experience – with all its drama, displaying God's power and glory – and after the rains came, Jezebel, King Ahab's wife, was enraged! So Elijah ran for his life, ending up in a cave. He was desperate and afraid. But the Lord came to him, reassuring the prophet of his presence. He told Elijah to go out and stand on the mountain, and to wait for the Lord to pass by.

A great wind came, but the Lord was not in it. An earthquake followed, but the Lord wasn't in that either. Nor was the Lord in the fire. Then Elijah heard a still small voice. God's voice. Just for him. He told Elijah to return, and God would provide for him. There would be 7,000 Israelites with him. But even more than this, God would select a prophet to succeed him – Elisha.

Elijah obeyed that 'still small voice' and later found his heir:

So he departed from there, and found Elisha … Then Elijah passed by him and threw his mantle on him (v 19 NKJV).

We may not use Siri on a regular basis to obtain information on our iPhones, if we have them. But we must *all* listen daily to God's still small voice as he speaks to us – being obedient and faithful, doing whatever he asks of us. So now, let's stop for a moment and listen very carefully. Do we hear him speaking? And, of utmost importance, what is he saying to us?

The Downward Spiral

All day long the battle raged, and the king was propped up in his chariot facing the Arameans … and that evening he died (22:35).

King Ahab's life illustrates how consistent disobedience leads to a tragic downward spiral. Even though he witnessed God's power on Mount Carmel, he refused to seek God's guidance against the attacking Aramean army. Twice God gave Ahab victory, yet Ahab responded by sparing the enemy's king – in disobedience to the Lord's command. Because of this, the king's life was taken.

We cannot begin to comprehend some portions of the Old Testament – especially when God commands his people to kill others for the sake of their survival. But we *can* understand what consistent disobedience is all about because we see it all around us. In fact, some of us have been caught up in the downward spiral ourselves.

When the Arameans attacked Israel, God wanted to assure King Ahab, once again, that he was with him and for him:

'This is what the LORD says … "I will deliver this vast army into your hands, and you will know that I am the LORD"' (20:28).

But only after Ahab was mortally wounded did he learn his lesson; and then it was too late. Yet it's never too late for us. Although Satan would love to pull us down, we must confess our sins – those known and also those of which we are not even aware – coming before God in all humility.

We close with a prayer I shared in as part of a congregation gathered for united worship at St Paul's Cathedral in London, England.

PRAYER
'Almighty God, our Heavenly Father, we have sinned against you, and against our neighbour – in thought, word and deed – through negligence and weakness, through our own deliberate fault. We are truly sorry and repent of all our sins. For the sake of your Son Jesus Christ, who died for us, forgive us all that is past; and grant that we may serve you in newness of life to the glory of your name. Amen.' (from the Church of England's *Book of Common Prayer*).

Hosanna in the Highest!

'Hosanna! Blessed is he who comes in the name of the Lord! Blessed is the coming kingdom of our father David! Hosanna in the highest!' (vv 9-10).

In his Gospel, Mark speaks to the mission of Jesus: his ministry of preaching and teaching in relation to the masses. Parables told; miracles performed; healings taking place. But the Gospel also outlines how the Lord mentored his twelve disciples. It was to them he revealed his ultimate destiny: his impending death, his glorious resurrection. Then the day came for a fulfilment of prophesy:

> *Rejoice greatly, O Daughter of Zion! Shout, Daughter of Jerusalem! See, your king comes to you, righteous and having salvation, gentle and riding on a donkey, on a colt, the foal of a donkey (Zechariah 9:9).*

Mark devotes over a third of his book to the last week of Jesus' life – the passion narrative, beginning with Jesus' royal procession into Jerusalem as King. The crowd welcomed him, rejoiced over him, shouted out their hosannas to him, for they thought he had come to liberate them from Roman oppression at last!

Nearly 200 years earlier, the Syrians had been trying to abolish all Jewish traditions. But in 167 BC a powerful Jewish leader, Judas Maccabeus, drove them all out – helping to re-establish his people spiritually by consecrating the Temple to the Lord. When they saw Jesus on the donkey, and threw down their cloaks and palm branches in front of him, perhaps they were hoping for another emancipator.

Yet Jesus came to save them from their sins. To free them, not from Roman oppression but from Satan's hold on them. To lead them into eternal life! Yes, the people shouted, 'Hosanna in the highest!' But they soon turned on him, scorned him, crucified him.

PRAYER
Lord God Almighty, I praise and bless you today. Help me to remain faithful to you – my King, my Saviour, my Lord!

The Greatest Commandment(s)

'The most important one,' answered Jesus, 'is this: "… Love the Lord your God with all your heart and with all your soul and with all your mind and with all your strength." The second is this: "Love your neighbour as yourself." There is no commandment greater than these' (vv 29-31).

The chief priests, elders, Pharisees and Sadducees were all hostile whenever they questioned Jesus – trying to catch him in going against the Law, in order to bring accusations of blasphemy against him. But the Scripture for today tells of a scribe coming to Jesus, simply asking him which of all the commandments was the most crucial.

Jesus responded by saying the most important was, primarily, one of the *heart*. We are to love God supremely. In Hebrew culture the heart was thought of as the centre of one's being. To love God with all of one's *heart* meant to allow God to rule all that we are.

Then Jesus added a second commandment, coming from the first: to love *others*. For it is not enough to love God alone; we are obliged to love our fellow human beings. How? As we love *ourselves*. Not a self 'love-in'; not self-centredness. But to treat others with love and respect, as we would want to be treated.

How then can we fulfil God's commandment(s) to love well?

*Love – **in the morning**.* We are to commence the day by giving it to the Lord; telling him we love him, wanting to live for him in all we say and do. Then asking him to bring to mind those who need extra love through encouragement – and promising to do so.

*Love – **during the in-between times**.* Any day might bring pressure, stress; various problems can arise. One author puts it this way: 'In-between the morning and the evening … This is where we all live most of the time. If our faith does not meet us in these times, then our religion is, for all practical purposes, pretty useless.'[4] We are trusting God – in faith, in love; and caring for others by loving them.

*Love – **in the evening**.* When the sun sets, we're to express our love to God in thanks for having been with us; for carrying us through. Then pray for those who need an extra touch of God's love.

PRAYER
I love you, God, with all my heart! Help me, *always*, to love others well.

Distress Call

Hasten, O God, to save me; O LORD, come quickly to help me (v 1).

There are people in the world who try to mess with us, and they may cause us to doubt. Some might make mockery of our faith. When we are young, sometimes it's hard to stand up to these kinds of jibes coming from others because we want to fit in, be accepted. For some young people, it might lead them to go astray.

David was a grown man when he wrote this psalm. Yet he still found it hard when people mocked him by saying, 'Aha! Aha!' (v 3) – perhaps poking fun at him. They were definitely out to pull him down, and even destroy him. So David did what came to him first. He sent a distress call to God: 'Hasten!' then 'Come quickly!' He knew he could not stand up to these individuals on his own. David needed God's help – and he needed it right away.

Have you ever put out a 'distress call' to God? I have, *many* times. Moments when I knew I could not make it in my own strength; when I was presented with difficult circumstances. Only God could save me. Yet sometimes we foolishly think God may be too busy for us, or even not available to come at our beck and call. But he is *always* willing to hear from us and come to our aid. We just have to put our faith and trust in him as we face each and every situation life presents.

David then tells us something wonderful. When we *do* send out that distress call, when we place our lives in the Lord's hands, we will then have great joy – desiring to praise our Lord and Deliverer:

But may all who seek you rejoice and be glad in you; may those who love your salvation always say, 'Let God be exalted!' (v 4).

So go ahead, if you need to. Send that distress call, asking God to be with you right now. *Together*, you will be able to face whatever lies ahead. With confidence, then say to the Father:

You are my help and my deliverer (v 5).

He will *never* let us down!

In my Life, Lord

Having believed, you were marked in him with a seal ... to the praise of his glory (vv 13-14).

Our song for today was written by American-born singer-songwriter Bob Kilpatrick in 1978. When interviewed about how this song came to be, he said he wrote it as a prayer – just to be sung by his wife Cindy and himself. *Their* song of consecration. It was never intended for the public – therefore, as Bob stated, there is a purity and intimacy about it.

When Cindy heard it, and sang it with her husband, she said many others would *also* be blessed by this beautiful song. So, it was published for us all:

> In my life, Lord, Be glorified ... Be glorified today.
> (*SASB* 593 v 1)

These lyrics are so powerful! Therefore, we must ask ourselves: Do we long for Jesus to be glorified in and through our lives? Not just for us individually, but also for our corps, our churches – or should we say, more correctly, *God's* corps and *God's* churches:

> In your Church, Lord, Be glorified ... Be glorified today.[5]
> (v 2)

How can the Lord be glorified in our lives? And in God's corps and churches? By being faithful to him. By upholding holiness. By following his will. By loving and caring for others. By being the people the Lord wants us to be – every moment of every day.

Do we *truly* want Christ to be glorified in us – today? Are we completely open to his leading, his direction? If so, can we join our voices to sing this beautiful, intimate song of commitment and dedication? Listen! Can we hear the voices of others around the world, consecrating themselves to Jesus?

God's Mouthpiece

The company of the prophets from Jericho, who were watching, said, 'The spirit of Elijah is resting on Elisha' (v 15).

The author of 2 Kings covers a period of about 300 years. In Israel, in the north, we have 19 wicked kings who consistently bring their people further and further away from the Lord. They are finally conquered by the Assyrians. In the south, Judah lasts about 150 years longer, but in the end, because of corrupt leadership, they also reap a bitter harvest – resulting in 70 years of exile in Babylon. Over these next few weeks, as we scan this disheartening time in the nation's history, we witness the last days of Israel and Judah.

The second chapter records Elijah and Elisha walking together, sharing together. Elijah knows his time on earth is about to end and shares this with Elisha, who responds by saying:

'Let me inherit a double portion of your spirit' (v 9).

Right after, a chariot of fire – with horses also of fire – appears, taking Elijah up to Heaven 'in a whirlwind' (v 11). What a sight that must have been! But then, Elisha notices something. He stoops down, picking up the cloak that had fallen from Elijah. He cries out, asking where God was in all of this:

Then he took the cloak that had fallen from him and struck the water with it. 'Where now is the LORD, the God of Elijah?' he asked. When he struck the water, it divided to the right and to the left, and he crossed over (v 14).

A miracle took place – witnessed by not only Elisha but also all the prophets from Jericho. It was a clear indication that the spirit of Elijah now rested upon Elisha. From then on he was to be God's mouthpiece for God's people.

God calls *all* of us to be his mouthpiece: to speak truth and love, into the lives of others. Are we willing to take up the mantle?

'Being there' for Others

'How can I help you?' (v 2).

While Elijah's ministry was generally characterised by large public acts and events, Elisha's spiritual leadership was mostly done in private as he focused on the needs of individuals.

In today's Scripture we read of a poor widow with many debts, and she feared her sons would be taken as slaves – for compensation. After approaching Elisha with her dilemma, he asked how he could help. She replied that all she had was a little oil, so the prophet told her to go to her neighbours – asking for empty jars. *Many* jars! She was then instructed to pour oil into them. She poured, and poured *more*. There was enough oil to pay off all her debts. A miracle!

Elisha then travelled with his servant Gehazi to Shunem, where he met and was warmly welcomed by a 'well-to-do' couple (v 8). He was so grateful that he said to the woman:

'Now what can be done for you?' (v 13).

This Shunammite woman desperately wanted a son, as her husband was old. Elisha promised that this would come true – and it did. Another miracle!

Elisha moved on. But after some time had elapsed, the boy became sick and died. Devastated, the woman set out to find the man of God. She pleaded with Elisha to return with her. When the prophet came to the place where the boy lay dead, he breathed life into him. A further miracle!

We might not have the public persona of Elijah; we might not have the same gift of performing miracles Elisha possessed. But we can *all* do wonderful and meaningful things for others to help them in their time of need. We can offer them hope, comfort, strength, friendship, encouragement. Are we willing to put ourselves on the line, daily, in order to *be there* for others – no matter what the cost?

PRAYER
Lord God, use me to help and bless others – in your holy name.

Believing, Behaving, Belonging

'If only my master would see the prophet who is in Samaria! He would cure him of his leprosy' (v 3).

People join religious congregations for many reasons. But perhaps the most common are these three: believing, behaving, belonging. In the Christian context, *believing* is usually the main priority. People want to exercise their faith in God, so belief in him is fundamental. Once someone accepts Christ as Saviour, they realise *behaviour* needs to be changed. And this is helped by interacting with others and *belonging* to a community of believers.

From today's Scripture we learn that Naaman – commander of the Syrian army, an enemy of Israel – has leprosy. An Israelite girl, captured and taken to be a servant of Naaman's wife, tells her mistress that a prophet of God in Israel can cure Naaman of his affliction. So the king of Aram (Syria) despatches his commander to the king of Israel. Elisha hears of this, sending the king a message:

'Make the man come to me' (v 8).

When Naaman arrived at Elisha's house, the prophet told him to go and wash himself seven times in the Jordan River. Naaman thought this to be foolishness. He was angry, full of rage. But his servants persuaded him to go to the river – and there, Naaman was healed. A miracle! He even declared:

'Now I know that there is no God in all the world except in Israel' (v 15).

It all began with a young slave girl believing in God and then sharing her belief with another person. Naaman even made a confession of belief. Hopefully his behaviour would change and, in time, he would find other believers so he could belong to a God-fearing fellowship.

The majority of us reading *Words of Life* are believers. We must make sure our behaviour is in line with our claim as Christians, and to always value belonging to the amazing family of God!

The Wanderers

'The spirit truly is ready, but the flesh is weak' (v 38 KJV).

More and more people are becoming inflicted with either the terrible disease of Alzheimer's or other forms of dementia. Statistics tell us that six in 10 people caught up in this state of confusion become lost at least once. They wander off, not sure where they are heading – creating great concern for those who love them.

I vividly recall, about 25 years ago, helping one of my children with their piano practice when – suddenly – I looked up, and there was an elderly man sitting in our living room. Not to startle him (as he had done to me!) I asked him who he was. He told me his name, saying this was his home. I gently took him out of the front door and was soon met by a frantic daughter wondering where her father had strayed to from *their* home.

People with any kind of dementia cannot help the 'wandering'. It's part of this heartbreaking disease. But let us think for a moment; have we ever caught ourselves *wandering* in our spiritual journey? We might think we know where we are heading – towards something enticing, something that is luring us away. But we do not really know where the road will take us. And once *there* – often stumbling, even falling – we're not sure how to get back.

Jesus told his disciples to look out, to watch, then to pray. If they didn't, they might 'enter into temptation' (v 38 *KJV*). As his followers, we are to be careful; to resist what might seem to be appealing. 'The flesh' *is* weak.

We can only resist all Satan's cunning ways to trip us up by asking the Holy Spirit to help us be intentional in resisting temptation. Are we committed, daily, to pray for God's strength?

PRAYER
Lord, I don't want to be a 'wanderer' in my spiritual journey with you. Keep me spiritually focused and committed to daily praying for your power in resisting all temptation.

The Empty Tomb

When Jesus rose early on the first day of the week, he appeared first to Mary Magdalene, out of whom he had driven seven demons (v 9).

Women, in Jesus' day, were not regarded as credible witnesses in Jewish courts. Why, then, did Jesus first appear to a woman, to Mary – who also had quite a reputation? Even when she went to those she knew well, the disciples could not accept her news:

… they did not believe it (v 11).

But later, when they saw Christ for themselves, they *did* believe! Yes, the empty tomb is all about God's marvellous story. It's his 'comment' on the Crucifixion. When Jesus cried out to his Father on the Cross, God gave his response on Easter morning. He did not abandon his Son! The empty tomb authenticates the ministry of Jesus, his complete obedient submission to suffering:

'Yet not what I will, but what you will' (Mark 14:36).

For certain, the empty tomb completely transformed the disheartened disciples – making them willing to follow Jesus' command:

'Go into all the world and preach the good news to all creation' (16:15).

Christ comes to us – asking what we are willing to do in response to the empty tomb. We all have a 'reputation' of sorts, but as believers we have been washed in the blood of the Lamb. And so, are we ready to share the good news of Jesus?

Prayer
Help me, Lord, to spread the wonderful news of the empty tomb; of your marvellous grace and your amazing love for *all* people!

A Continual Feast

The tongue that brings healing is a tree of life (v 4).

King Solomon speaks much about the tongue in his writings. As we know, words expressed can do great damage: gossip, slander, anger. The tongue can cut someone down in moments, creating such havoc in our relationships with others – especially those close to us. But the good news is this: the tongue can be such an instrument of grace, peace, kindness, love – adding soothing oil to the bitter effects of a tongue that is uncontrolled. So how can we use our tongue in an effective way?

Speaking truth. The tongue can help bring the truth of God's love to others. We can share our testimony, telling people how the Lord has changed *our* lives; give truthful counsel when needed; communicate the reality of God's transformational power.

Giving encouragement. When someone encourages us, it lifts our spirit. We are to do likewise:

… how good is a timely word! (v 23).

Perhaps it's a word to encourage someone going through a difficult time. Or we share the good news of God's love with people who have a particular need:

… good news gives health to the bones (v 30).

Expressing joy. As we express our joy with others, our facial expression changes. We smile; we laugh; we celebrate life, because:

… the cheerful heart has a continual feast (v 15).

I love this verse! It reminds us all that we can celebrate, together, in 'a continual feast' of the Lord's abiding presence. Even today, are we willing to use our tongue, our words, to share something of Jesus' love with others? If we do, we will *feast* with others around the world. It can't get much better than this!

Jehovah is our Strength

'The LORD is my strength and my song' (v 2).

Trials and temptations come to us all – and sometimes, seemingly, out of nowhere. Satan would love to pull us down. But God is 'stronger than his foes' and will help us when we call out to him:

> Jehovah is our strength, And he shall be our song;
> We shall o'ercome at length Although our foes be strong.
> In vain does Satan then oppose, For God is stronger than his foes.
>
> (*SASB* 38 v 1)

Samuel Barnard, who died in 1807, was a minister and also composed several hymns. It's thought today's song is one of them. We say this because in 1799 he submitted several of his hymns anonymously into a compilation entitled *Spiritual Songs for Zion's Travellers*.

He originally wrote the hymn in the first person but later it was changed to be more inclusive – for the Lord is indeed *our* refuge and has made *all* of us his:

> The Lord our refuge is And ever will remain;
> Since he has made us his He will our cause maintain.
> In vain our enemies oppose, For God is stronger than his foes.
>
> (v 2)

The final verse reminds us that our names are written on the heart of God. How beautiful! How reassuring. He is with us, and we are promised he will never leave us. With a sense of confidence and strength, given to us by God alone, let us join our voices in singing this final verse together as our united testimony:

> Our God our Father is; Our names are on his heart;
> We ever will be his, He ne'er from us will part.
> In vain the mightiest powers oppose,
> For God is stronger than his foes.

Open my Eyes, Lord!

'Set food and water before them so that they may eat and drink and then go back to their master' (v 22).

The Arameans, at war with Israel, planned an ambush. Elisha, aware of this plot, warned the king of Israel. The king of Aram then demanded to know where the prophet of Israel resided. Once informed, the enemy troops surrounded the city of Dothan.

When Elisha's servant saw all the horses and chariots surrounding them, he became frantic. But Elisha was calm – knowing the Lord was with them. He prayed that his servant would see God at work:

'O LORD, open his eyes so that he may see' (v 17).

As the horses and chariots came towards them, Elisha prayed again – that *their* eyes would be struck with blindness. God led the enemy to Samaria, where the king of Israel was established. When the enemies' eyes were opened, they knew they were trapped. The king of Israel then asked Elisha if he should kill them all.

Elisha responded in an unusual way by telling the king to shower them with kindness instead. So they gave the enemy water and food – and then sent them all home! The eyes of the king of Israel were opened that day, coming to realise that treating the enemy with compassion would prevent further invasion of their land:

So the bands from Aram stopped raiding Israel's territory (v 23).

God is constantly at work in ways we cannot see. The eyes of Elisha's servant were opened – seeing God at work. The eyes of the king of Israel were opened – to see that kindness benefited all concerned. May *our* eyes be continually opened to see God at work in marvellous ways, in our lives and in the lives of others. And may this realisation bring glory to our living and gracious God!

Influence and Intercession

'Then take the flask and pour the oil on his head and declare, "This is what the LORD says: I anoint you king over Israel"' (v 3).

Some 10-12 years previous to our Scripture passage for today, King Jehoshaphat of Judah wooed the friendship of King Ahab in Israel (see 1 Kings chapter 22) in an attempt to join forces against Syria. But the alliance with Ahab caused God's people to adopt his wicked practices. Ahab's wife Jezebel, and all their family, were also involved in Baal worship – soon embraced by the Israelites themselves. God rebuked Judah and Israel for their idolatry, but both the northern and southern kingdoms continued in their evil ways.

It was now time to cleanse the nations of Ahab's descendants. Through Elisha, God told Jehu – commander of Israel's army – it was his task to persevere:

> *'"You are to destroy the house of Ahab your master, and I will avenge the blood of my servants … The whole house of Ahab will perish … As for Jezebel, dogs will devour her … and no one will bury her"' (vv 7-8, 10).*

Pretty stark! Sometimes passages in the Old Testament are difficult to comprehend. Here we find Jehu, seemingly quite cruel, to be used by God – in order to wipe out the wicked house of Ahab. And the commander would even be 'rewarded' by becoming king.

What's the bottom line? Sin will not be tolerated by Holy God. What we do, good or bad, does affect us – and even the generations that follow us. So, what are we doing to positively impact those who come after us? Not just our own children, but *all* those of younger generations. Are we living holy, God-honouring lives?

ACTION
Let's make contact with someone younger than ourselves, telling them we are praying for them and are available to talk if they wish to share with us. God will honour our influence and prayers of intercession.

Missio Dei

They anointed him, and the people clapped their hands and shouted, 'Long live the king!' (v 12).

A hab's family were all killed, including the wicked Jezebel. The ministers of Baal were also wiped out, to the point of Baal worship being destroyed in Israel (see 2 Kings 10:28). Yet Jehu was not careful in keeping God's law; nor were those who succeeded him.

Then, a bright spot – found in the southern kingdom of Judah. After King Ahaziah's death, his mother Athaliah usurped the throne – by killing all the royal heirs. However, baby Joash was saved by a courageous nurse who hid him at the temple of the Lord for six years. When he became king – ruling for 40 years – Joash was known to be one of the greatest reforming kings in Judah.

Missio Dei is a Latin phrase which means the 'mission of God'. For King Joash this 'mission' meant several things: repairing the Temple that had been long neglected; bringing the people back to God; rededicating themselves to God's purpose; re-establishing their covenant by destroying all idols and all Baal temples.

What does *Missio Dei* mean for *us*? May I suggest some possibilities:

Reaching out to people who desperately need Christ.
Refocusing our time and energy, to be used mightily by God.
Rededicating ourselves to God's service in very practical ways.
Recommitting our covenant with God in a very personal way.
Restoring God's joy, peace, love – within ourselves and in others.

King Joash was the leader of God's people. *We* are all leaders – as we strive to lead others to Christ daily. May our personal *Missio Dei*, as well as our corporate mission, be to bring others to Jesus.

PRAYER

'Dear Lord, let me share the good news of your Son Jesus. Let the life that I live and the words that I speak be a witness to my faith in him. And let me share the story of my salvation with others so that they, too, might receive his eternal gifts. Amen.'[6]

Spiritual Blindness

'What? Are we blind too?' (v 40).

As I write these words for today, I have an appointment with my optometrist later this afternoon. She will check my eyesight and let me know if I need to take any action concerning my sight. Our eyes are so important! Yet statistics tell us – at least in North America – someone goes blind every 20 minutes. Perhaps it's similar where you live, or possibly the statistic is even worse.

In John chapter 9 we read of a man being born blind. Yesterday, I chatted with a man connected with our church who was born blind. You no doubt know someone inflicted with blindness, someone never having seen God's glorious creation, never having gazed upon the faces of family and friends they love. But for the man in John's Gospel, Jesus changed everything. He gave him *sight*:

'One thing I do know. I was blind but now I see!' (v 25).

But the *greater* miracle was the opening of his heart to the Saviour:

Then the man said, 'Lord, I believe,' and he worshipped him (v 38).

The man's *spiritual* eyes were suddenly opened to see the Son of Man for who he was. But the Pharisees didn't get it, questioning Jesus – in a sarcastic way – if they too were blind. They were! Theirs was a *spiritual blindness*. So their guilt remained.

Many people today claim they 'see' and know what truth is all about. Yet they are blinded to it – because of pride, self-righteousness, even traditions. Blinded to *the* truth of who the Son of God really is: 'The light of the world'! (9:5).

PRAYER
Lord, help me never to be blinded by pride or selfishness. I want to *see* you, for who you really are, in all your majesty and glory!

His Voice

'My sheep listen to my voice; I know them, and they follow me' (v 27).

Voice recognition, for the most part, is a wonderful thing. Of course, there are some voices we do not want to hear – those of people who have hurt us, caused us great pain. But to answer our phone, then hear the distinctive and unique voice of someone we know and love and cherish, brings such warmth to the heart! We feel a sense of comfort, of security, for we know the person at the other end wants to talk to us and share something with us.

Even the sound of a familiar voice coming from another room in the same house brings joy to one's soul. Or it could be the voices of little children; the voices of a beautiful choir; the voices of people laughing together. And to *recognise* the voice is to know something of the character of the individual speaking, singing – even laughing.

Today's incident happened during the Feast of Dedication, commemorating the rededication of the Temple – originally established by Judas Maccabeus in 164 BC. Jesus was in the Temple courts when the Jews asked him if he really was the Christ. Jesus had told them he was, but they didn't believe him. Why? Because they were not part of his fold. Not his sheep. Only those who believed in him, who had faith in the Shepherd, were part of his flock. And his sheep knew him because they knew his *voice* – having a loving, living, lasting relationship with their Shepherd.

Let's pause for a moment, taking time to *listen*. Then, let's ask the Lord to speak to us – and wait to hear his voice. Most likely it will not be audible. But we *will* hear him. What is he saying to us right now? To do something? To speak with someone or contact them? Listen. Be still. Wait… Now, what else do we hear him saying?

PRAYER

Lord, I must admit, sometimes my life gets pretty hectic; I fail to stop and slow down, just to *listen*. Speak, Lord. I *do* want to hear your voice, right now. I am ready, and willing, to obey – whatever you ask of me.

The Mouth

My mouth will tell of your righteousness, of your salvation all day long (v 15).

Have you ever heard the expression, 'Straight from the horse's mouth'? We would not want to repeat this phrase to a colleague when our superior has just told us something – and certainly not if they are still nearby!

The phrase actually comes from the early 1900s and is said to do with the selling of horses. A dealer could try to twist the truth of a horse's age, but the evidence was right inside the horse's mouth. Its teeth determined its age, and this gauge was completely reliable every time.

Some Christians say they are not good with telling others about Jesus. They would rather just 'live the life'. It's true, we must live according to God's holy standards. But we must also *tell* others about Jesus – by using the mouth God has given us. If we are living a holy life, what we say *will* be reliable and authentic.

When are we required to tell others of God's righteousness? Right from the beginning:

Since my youth, O God, you have taught me, and to this day I declare your marvellous deeds (v 17).

And if we are somewhat older:

Even when I am old and grey, do not forsake me, O God, till I declare your power to the next generation (v 18).

We are *all* to use our mouth to tell others of Jesus. How else will they hear the good news of salvation? Of the hope that can be theirs if they put their trust in him? We may not tell them that what we share comes from the horse's mouth; but they *should* be able to tell that what does come out of our mouth is absolute truth, that God loves every one of us and wants to claim us as his own.

May each one of us use our mouth to tell others of Jesus daily:

My tongue will tell of your righteous acts all day long (v 24).

Fairest Lord Jesus

In him everything in heaven and on earth was created, not only things visible but also the invisible orders of thrones, sovereignties, authorities, and powers: the whole universe has been created through him and for him (v 16 NEB).

This is definitely one of my favourite hymns! Maybe it's yours also. I love this song because it extols the beauty of Jesus our Lord, the One we cherish and honour:

> Fairest Lord Jesus, Lord of all nature,
> O thou of God and man the Son;
> Thee will I cherish, Thee will I honour,
> Thou my soul's glory, joy and crown.
> *(SASB* 77 v 1)

Little is known about this extraordinary hymn. Some think it was composed by German crusaders in the 12th century, when travelling to the Holy Land. Others believe it was written much later. Whatever the case, it speaks of the beauty of creation – yet Jesus is fairer than all:

> Fair are the meadows, Fairer the woodlands,
> Robed in the blooming garb of spring;
> Jesus is fairer, Jesus is purer,
> Who makes the woeful heart to sing.
> (v 2)

What we know for certain is that our beautiful Saviour is supreme and is Lord of all. As we give glory, honour, praise and adoration to him, let's sing together this final verse – worshipping him and affirming our deep love for him this day:

> Beautiful Saviour, Lord of the nations,
> Son of God and Son of Man,
> Glory and honour, Praise, adoration,
> Now and for evermore be thine.

Trust

Hezekiah trusted in the LORD, the God of Israel (18:5).

Taking the throne at the age of 25, Hezekiah soon established himself as perhaps the greatest reformer Judah had seen. He began by destroying all traces of heathen worship – choosing to put all his trust in God alone. Yet after a certain period of time, Hezekiah became very ill. After praying about this, God responded:

'I will add fifteen years to your life' (20:6).

It was all about trust. Trusting God for the present and for the future. Some people find it hard to trust, perhaps having been hurt, betrayed – often by people they once had trusted. Once the trust has been violated, it is hard to trust again.

There are many people we *can* trust, however. This is a wonderful thing, to have family and friends we can depend upon. And hopefully *we* can be trusted. I think of my young grandchildren. They trust Grandma implicitly – knowing I will keep them, to the very best of my ability, from any impending harm.

Yes, we all – as God's children – must be people of integrity; people of our word. Trustworthy. But best of all, God can be trusted. Fully! When we put our trust in the Lord, he will work out all things in our lives – according to his perfect plan and purpose.

Hezekiah trusted God:

- He did what was right in the eyes of the LORD (18:3);
- He trusted in the LORD the God of Israel (18:5);
- He didn't cease from following God (18:6).

The Lord was with Hezekiah (18:7) and, because of his trust, Hezekiah was successful in all he did (18:7).

What a testimony to a great man of God! Can people give such a testimony about us? With the Holy Spirit's help, and with our eyes focused on God alone, may it be so for each one of us.

Not to the Right, Not to the Left

Josiah was eight years old when he became king … He kept straight on the path blazed by his ancestor David, not one step to either left or right (22:1-2 MSG).

Following Hezekiah's death several kings sent Judah into spiritual chaos. Godlessness! Then, at the young age of eight, Josiah came to the throne – following his evil father Amon and his wicked grandfather Manasseh. So how could such a terrible father and grandfather produce a young man, Josiah, who was not only *good* but who loved the Lord too?

Josiah was a gracious gift from God who did not turn 'to either left or right'. Even when he was a 16-year-old teenager, Josiah sought after the things of God:

In the eighth year of his reign, while he was still young, he began to seek the God of his father David (2 Chronicles 34:3).

It is so easy to get off track. Things on our 'right' – calling out to us, luring us away from the path God has set for us. Things on our 'left' – enticing us. Why not go try them out? Explore a bit?

Josiah kept focused. By doing this, and not straying from God, he managed to do the following:

- He purged Judah from idol worship (see 2 Chronicles 34:33);
- He began repairing the Temple – finding the Book of the Law, which was then reintroduced to God's people;
- He brought God's people to a place of recommitment, a renewal of their covenant with Almighty God.

Something, even some*one*, may try to steer us off course in our spiritual journey. Let us make sure our eyes remain fixed on Jesus!

Action
As we look around us today, seeing what's on our right and on our left, let's thank God for the path he has just for me and just for you. It's the only one that will lead us to ultimate victory!

What's the Verdict?

So Judah went into exile out of its land (v 21 NRSV).

Soon after Josiah's death, God poured out his long-delayed judgement upon Judah. The nation's persistent idolatry and immorality could no longer be tolerated. God used a foreign king and his powerful army to sweep over the land. Nebuchadnezzar, along with his troops from Babylon, captured Jerusalem, bringing destruction, death and then deportation.

Everything of value in the city of Jerusalem was first removed, then the city was burned. Devastation! The walls were levelled. The once-glorious kingdom was disintegrated. And from then on, even though the Jews were restored to their homeland after 70 years of exile, nothing would ever be the same again. In the words of Isaiah the prophet, Judah would not rise again until the Lord came to re-establish it:

> *In days to come the mountain of the LORD'S house shall be established …*
> *all the nations shall stream to it (Isaiah 2:2 NRSV).*

For Judah, judgement had to take place for there to be any sense of holiness and purity and eventual restoration. What about us? True, we may not blatantly sin against God. But things can creep into our lives that are not good, aren't holy. Or maybe we miss opportunities God has for us, because we're too comfortable in our faith.

I'm certain for us all, when we are presented before the Almighty, we will long to hear God declare his verdict, saying we have been 'faithful'!

PONDER
'A single grateful thought raised to Heaven is the most perfect prayer' (Gotthold Ephraim Lessing, 1729-1781)**. Let us raise to Heaven our thoughts of gratefulness – all day long!**

Boundless Blessings!

Reflections on the 150th anniversary International Congress

The following is a short series of reflections from *Boundless – The Whole World Redeeming*, the International Congress of The Salvation Army held 1-5 July last year to celebrate 150 years of service to nations around the globe. Whether or not we are Salvationists, I pray these writings will bless and inspire us in our faith journey with the Lord.

I have included a 'prelude' as people gathered from many countries on 30 June; also a 'postlude' – thoughts following the close of the congress relating to what is next for us as God's people.

Before writing, I sensed the Lord wanting to give me one word for each day: a word to hold on to which would help us live according to God's will. Then, as the congress began, I soon came to realise that two songs were predominant throughout the meetings. Of course, the first, written by William Booth, is what has become known as the Founder's song: 'O Boundless Salvation!'. The second comes from the musical *The Blood of the Lamb* by Generals John Gowans and John Larsson: 'They Shall Come from the East, They Shall Come from the West'. Both of these powerful, inspirational songs are referenced in this series.

Those who attended the congress – some 15,000 Salvationists representing (as I now write) 127 countries where the Army has a presence – were richly blessed and strangely stirred in their hearts. This is something not always easy to put into words. Yet I pray, as we move through these next few days together, that God the Father will be ever-present; that we will feel the Son speaking to us personally; and that we will be fully aware of the Spirit blessing us in unexpected ways.

May each one of us know God's *boundless* love, and may we all be inspired and then motivated to reach out to a world that desperately needs the Saviour!

B.I.

They Shall Come …

And I heard a loud voice from the throne saying, 'Now the dwelling of God is with men, and he will live with them. They will be his people, and God himself will be with them and be their God (v 3).

There is so much excitement in the air. It's electric! A sense of such great anticipation; a real buzz. It's 'the day before'. A day when people are gathering from all corners of the earth, not just to celebrate The Salvation Army but above all to give praise and honour to Jesus. Plans for this great international congress have been in the working for several years, and the reality is finally taking place.

Today is the prelude. People are registering, getting acquainted with the huge facility where the gatherings are taking place in London, England – birthplace of The Salvation Army. It's the 'overture'. We are hearing all around us the beautiful music of voices, filled with great joy, before the symphonic work officially begins tomorrow.

So we ask: What are we expecting? What will this Salvationist symphony 'sound' like over the next five days? What are we anticipating that will inspire, motivate, encourage and bless us all for the days to come – and beyond?

Wonderful Music. The Salvation Army is indeed blessed with good music! Whether it be instrumental, vocal or other forms of music, it will be thrilling to take it all in, and be richly blessed.

Rich Fellowship. We will meet friends we have known for years. But how wonderful to meet *new* people – from around the world!

Hearing from God. The Lord has convened this congress, I believe, because he wants to say something to us – corporately, individually.

Sensing the Presence of the Holy Spirit. Sprit of the living God, O yes, fall on us *all* we pray!

Being Surprised! What is God going to reveal to me? To you?

PRAYER
Father God, we thank you for raising up and blessing The Salvation Army for more than 150 years! Now, bless *me*, Lord Jesus. Keep me open and receptive to your Holy Spirit, I pray.

Clean Robes

'Blessed are those who wash their robes, that they might have the right to the tree of life and may go through the gates into the city' (v 14).

It's the first official day of the international congress. The first time more than 15,000 Salvationists are meeting in one place to worship together – along with thousands of others 'connected' through the means of online streaming of the congress around the world. What a gathering of God's people!

Earlier in the day Salvation Army officers were challenged by the General to be real and authentic: for each to experience and live out a life of holiness – out of love for Almighty God. If we want to one day enter the Kingdom of God, all of us *must* have clean robes:

> They shall come from the east, they shall come from the west,
> And sit down in the Kingdom of God;
> Both the rich and the poor, the despised, the distressed …
> And none will ask what they have been
> Provided that their robes are clean …
>
> (*SASB* 1011 v 1)

Us – in clean robes! Presented before God as pure, holy, Christlike. Amen!

*Word for the Day: **Boundless.*** It is the title of the congress, so we are to begin here! It's a word that speaks of God's unending love and grace; his boundless salvation for everyone. The word is for all of us gathered in London, and also for those at home or wherever else people find themselves. God's boundless love stretches out to people in our cities, our communities, to the person next door. God calls us to tell all men and women, boys and girls, of his boundless love – for *them*. Are we prepared to do this, for his sake?

As I write these words I look around the vast arena, thanking God for every individual; also for every person reading *Words of Life* today. May the Lord bless, keep, protect and use each of us for his glory. And may the Holy Spirit help us all to have clean robes.

I'll Fight!

Put on the full armour of God so that you can take your stand against the devil's schemes (v 11).

The terms 'social justice' and 'social action' are on the lips of so many these days. We almost think they are something new. But no; these ideas have been around for many years. A prime example is found in William Booth's last public address, delivered to his people on 9 May 1912 in the Royal Albert Hall, London – just months before his death: 'While women weep, as they do now, I'll fight! While little children go hungry, as they do now, I'll fight! While men go to prison, in and out, in and out, as they do now, I'll fight! While there is a drunkard left, while there is a lost girl upon the streets, while there remains one dark soul without the light of God, I'll fight – I'll fight to the very end!'

We are hearing many testimonies at the congress. They are given by and about people who have been greatly helped through the Army over the 150 years of its existence. Some tell of lives that have been completely transformed because Salvationists were obedient to God's call upon them.

What about us? Are *we* willing to 'fight' against the injustices of the world? Do we 'weep' when we see the marginalised mistreated? May God help us to be obedient to his call – now and always.

Word for the Day: **Bridge.** We were reminded brilliantly – by bridges being projected on the screens in the arena, and also through drama – that we are called to be God's servants, his 'priests'. The word priest comes from the Latin, *pontifex*, meaning bridge-builder. We are to be Christ for 'the whosoever'; to be a transforming influence for a world in desperate need of Jesus.

But we are not simply to be bridge-builders; we are to *be* those bridges. People available and ready to be Christ's hands and feet, wherever we find ourselves. To be bridges of peace and reconciliation. Are we open to God's leading?

PRAYER
Help me to be that bridge, Lord. And help me to fight the good fight – bringing justice for *all* people, for *your* sake.

O Boundless Salvation!

'For God so loved the world that he gave his one and only Son, that whoever believes in him shall not perish but have eternal life' (v 16).

On this third day of the congress we have been hearing and singing William Booth's song. It's a song that reminds us we have been redeemed, renewed, restored, released:

> O boundless salvation! deep ocean of love,
> O fullness of mercy, Christ brought from above,
> The whole world redeeming, so rich and so free,
> Now flowing for all men, come, roll over me!   (*SASB* 509 v 1)

Some 70 years later, another song was written – also originating from England, but from a far different perspective. In a famous Beatles' song, 'Eleanor Rigby', the question is asked: 'All the lonely people, where do they all come from?' We actually heard this tune played at the congress – reminding us there are so many men and women, boys and girls, who need to hear that God has come for *everyone* and that *they* can be saved!

We must get rid of any obstacles to people being able to hear the good news of Jesus – breaking down barriers of language, culture, status. For it's all about 'the whole world redeeming'. Yes, the world for God! No prejudice or judgement; no preconceived agendas. Rather, we fully embrace God's world with arms of love.

Word for the Day: **Light.** In the beginning there was darkness. Then God created light! And although there is still darkness in the world, Jesus has come as our Light. The congress delegates, wearing wristbands that lit up in the darkened arena at a specific moment, created a stunning brilliance! The effect was a vivid reminder that we are to *be* lights for others – each of us being a candle of the Lord permeating the ever-present darkness that surrounds us. No matter our age or situation, the question must be asked: Are we up for this challenge?

PRAYER
Help us to be your lights in our communities, O God – in order that redemption will come for the whole world.

Touching the Wave

'Therefore go and make disciples of all nations' (v 19).

The cacophony of brilliant, majestic sounds coming at us from such a variety of groups, individuals and mediums at the congress virtually takes one's breath away. And to know that they are all fragrant offerings of praise to God Almighty is almost overwhelming.

Today's gathering is all about honouring God for who he is and for all he has done – and is still doing – for us as The Salvation Army and as individuals within the Army. The mosaic of cultures represented in this session is a constant reminder that we *all* love the Army; but above all, that we are deeply in love with the One who raised up the Army – Jesus Christ!

The congress is inspiring us, more than ever before, to touch the 'wave' of a great tide:

> The tide is now flowing, I'm touching the wave,
> I hear the loud call of the mighty to save;
> My faith's growing bolder, delivered I'll be;
> I plunge 'neath the waters, they roll over me.   (*SASB* 509 v 6)

We are to not only listen to a call to reach men and women for the Lord, but also to obey that call. To strengthen our faith – to the point of taking the plunge and letting the waters roll over us.

Word for the Day: **Others.** The General said we must all 'fight for what is right'. Yet we live in a narcissistic world: people think only of themselves. They have no real care for others. One Christmas, not long before his death, William Booth sent a telegram to Salvationists around the world. The greeting contained only one word: 'Others!' He wanted his people to take the focus away from 'self' and give financially to the needy; to give of *themselves* to others – in every way possible. May this also be our mandate as we strive to point others to our Lord and Saviour, Jesus Christ.

PRAYER
Lord, I'm feeling invigorated and rejuvenated in my spirit, wanting to tell others about you. Let your Spirit's waves roll over me today!

The Rest of My Days

After this I heard what sounded like the roar of a great multitude in heaven shouting: 'Hallelujah! Salvation and glory and power belong to our God' (v 1).

No one knows the *quantity* of time we have left on earth; we have no real control over this. But we do have a say in the *quality* of our lives, what we are going to do with each moment granted to us. If we sing this final verse of the Founder's song with truthfulness, we choose to spend the rest of our days 'promoting' the praise of our Saviour with great joy in our hearts:

> And now, hallelujah! the rest of my days
> Shall gladly be spent in promoting his praise
> Who opened his bosom to pour out this sea
> Of boundless salvation for you and for me. (*SASB* 509 v 7)

As this final day of the congress is a Sunday, we gather for a very special and sacred time of worship. At one point we can hear someone singing the opening verse of the majestic hymn 'Holy, holy, holy, Lord God Almighty!'. Then, projected on the screen, we see and hear another joining in – and then another. Before long, *hundreds* of people from around the world are all singing this powerful hymn. All ages; all nationalities; from all walks of life. Words cannot express the emotions felt. Tears stream uncontrollably down my face. And I am not alone! A holy moment. A God moment. O yes, *boundless salvation* – for you, for me, for *all*!

Word for the Day: **Hallelujah!** The General stated: 'We are no better than anyone else, not superior to any person we serve.' We are simply God's people – called to battle against sin, and to reach out 'to the whosoever'. Are we prepared to win the world for Jesus – no matter the cost? To be, as the General also said, 'an Army on its knees'? A people promising to pray for the salvation of others – for the rest of our days? May this become a reality.

PRAYER
Holy God, we want to go forward promoting your praise. Keep us faithful, the rest of our days, so that one day we will all live together, with you, for ever. HALLELUJAH!

What Now?

'Consecrate yourselves, for tomorrow the Lord will do amazing things among you' (v 5).

It is the day after; perhaps an emotional let-down as people begin to disperse, heading home. A time when Satan no doubt begins to prowl – striving to pull people to *his* side. Yet we are on the Lord's side! We leave the congress renewed, re-energised – and on fire for God!

We have experienced wonderful singing, brass bands, vocalists, drama, a new musical, timbrelists and a myriad of other artistic presentations. We have spent these days praising the Lord in phenomenal ways! But what now? What does the future hold? William Booth once said: 'We are forming and fashioning generations yet unknown, and oh, I do rejoice in the fact that it is not what we are now, but what we shall be, that will fit us for the great work that God has for us to do.'

It's now a year later. How has the congress impacted us – whether we were there or not? What about the 'generations' to come? I believe God still loves The Salvation Army! He sees it doing great mission around the world. But it will only be as good as its members. So Christ asks us to be his hands and feet; to consecrate ourselves, fully, for his service. *Will* we? And if so, what can we do now and in the days to come?

Pray. We are to pray, daily, for not only the Army but the Church universal. That God will empower us all to reach others for Jesus.

Read God's Word. We must promise to read God's Word faithfully, every day, for he longs to speak to us corporately and individually.

Embrace holy living. It's essential that holiness is part of our lifestyle, part of who we are as God's people.

Reach out to others. We are to love and care for *all* people.

The Army's Founder also said (somewhat whimsically): 'If I thought I could win one more soul to the Lord by walking on my head and playing the tambourine with my toes, I'd learn how!' Are we willing to do anything, go anywhere – in order that we reach others for Jesus?

Boundless – The Whole World Redeeming. Yes, the world for God! Will we each do our part?

Prayer
Shine, Jesus, shine! Shine on your Army. Shine on us *all*!

Perfume

Then Mary took about a pint of pure nard, an expensive perfume; she poured it on Jesus' feet and wiped his feet with her hair (v 3).

Mary of Bethany is a woman every Christian should emulate. Each time she is mentioned in the Gospels, she is described as being at the feet of Jesus (see also Luke 10:39; John 11:32). In this position, perhaps it is more conducive to worshipping the Lord; to receive from him; to experience his comfort, care, compassion; to sense his extraordinary and extravagant love.

Kneeling at the feet of Jesus, Mary was willing to sacrifice her most costly possession. Her perfume was worth hundreds of dollars by today's standards. It could have been her dowry, in the hopes of a marriage proposal one day. But she took it, pouring it over the feet of her Master; then she wiped them with her hair. It was a love offering to the One she adored and worshipped.

Why did she do it? She had to do *something* in order to express her total devotion to her Saviour. Yes, it was a sacrifice. But that did not matter to Mary. She probably hadn't thought of it beforehand; but suddenly, she knew this was right. To give all she had. *Everything!*

What can we give to Jesus – in an act of selfless worship? Yes, we could offer money or buy something for our church. But we know that the most precious and treasured thing we can give is ourselves. To yield all that we *are* to Jesus – as our humble act of worship.

May I be bold enough to suggest we get on our knees right now, if we are able, and pour out the 'perfume' of our lives to the Lord in an act of rededication to him. And as we do this, *our* home will be:

… filled with the fragrance of the perfume (v 3).

Prayer
Lord Jesus, as I bow before you in humble adoration, I ask you to accept the 'perfume' of my love right now. Bless me and help me – each and every day – to be a fragrant blessing to others!

Feet

After that, he poured water into a basin and began to wash his disciples'
feet, drying them with the towel that was wrapped round him (v 5).

Saying goodbye is never easy, especially if we are saying it to family or
friends. Yet what we say or do in those few moments before leaving is
significant. We prepare ourselves, and those we care about, for a change.
We will be gone – although we usually try to figure out when we will be
together again in the future.

In John chapters 13-17, the Lord gives his 'farewell speech' to his
disciples – those who have been with him, day in and day out, for the past
three years. He commences by doing something quite unusual, yet so
important. He washes their feet. An object lesson they would never forget –
and nor should we.

It was an act of total humility. To wash feet. Feet that are dirty and no
doubt very smelly. Feet that are sometimes not perfectly formed,
awkward-looking, calloused and hardened. Feet that are private, unseen –
unlike hands, which are always exposed.

But Jesus rose from the supper table, poured water into a basin, took off
his outer garments, wrapped a towel around his waist, then stooped – bent
low – to wash his disciples' feet. It was the act of a lowly servant; an intimate
act of deep affection; an act of humility and grace – rebuking any sense of
selfishness or pride the disciples might have still possessed.

How profound! Our Lord takes the place of a servant. Bending low at
the feet of his followers. Washing and tenderly drying their feet on a towel.
He then tells them – and us:

'Now that I, your Lord and Teacher, have washed your feet, you also
should wash one another's feet' (v 14).

We are to serve others – as serving Jesus. To do so in all humility, out of
our deep love for our Lord.

PRAYER
Lord, I want to be your humble servant.

A Peaceful Kingdom

In His days the righteous shall flourish, and abundance of peace, until the moon is no more (v 7 NKJV).

Solomon was both king and son of a king. So is our Lord. He has all authority in himself, yet also is given royal authority by his Father. And one day he will come to reign on earth, in all his righteousness. All will be made right, for justice will rule. There will be *peace* in his Kingdom that will be lasting and eternal.

I recently read a beautiful story that is true and heart-warming. A newborn foal had been abandoned by his mother and seemed to be in great distress. The farmer, not quite knowing what to do, decided to bring a four-foot giant teddy bear into the foal's stall. There was an immediate attraction – a comforting replacement for the animal's mother. The foal nuzzled up to the bear's face during the day and slept across the teddy bear's feet at night. Peace.

We all long for a peaceful kingdom, a peaceful world. For a time when we can live beyond all the drama life presents. To surround ourselves with those who make us smile. To focus on the good and the holy, while treating one another with dignity and respect. To remember that falling down may be part of life, but getting back up is living – all in God's strength.

One day God will come to reign. Yes, his peaceful Kingdom will come and:

He will bring justice to the poor … he will save the children of the needy (v 4 NKJV).

But we can help be agents of peace *now*, to people in need of comfort. Being alongside others, helping to create an atmosphere of calm and goodness. Bringing something in a time of need. Letting people know of the peace Christ can bring into their hearts. Then we can sing together:

… blessed be His glorious name forever! And let the whole earth be filled with His glory. Amen and Amen (v 19 NKJV).

You Can't Stop Rain

How great is the love the Father has lavished on us, that we should be called children of God! (v 1).

There are many things we can prevent from happening, such as eating food that isn't good for us; watching television and using our computer too much; constantly checking out messages on our phone. But when it comes to the weather, or change of seasons, they are part of God's domain:

> You can't stop rain from falling down,
> Prevent the sun from shining,
> You can't stop spring from coming in,
> Or winter from resigning,
> Or still the waves or stay the winds,
> Or keep the day from dawning,
> You can't stop God from loving you,
> His love is new each morning.
> > (*SASB* 72 v 1)

Here, the late General John Gowans reminds us of the best news of all: no matter what we do, or do not do, we simply cannot stop God loving us! Isn't this amazing? We would never want to take advantage of this, or exploit God's promise to always love us in any way. And when we realise we're loved to this extent – knowing God *lavishes* his love upon us, and that his love is *new* every morning – we want to love him in return, with all our being.

Let's sing this last verse with great joy, because of God's love – for *ever*!

> You can't stop God from loving you
> Though you may disobey him,
> You can't stop God from loving you,
> However you betray him;
> From love like this no power on earth
> The human heart can sever,
> You can't stop God from loving you,
> Not God – not now, nor ever.

Character

'Those who survived the exile and are back in the province are in great trouble and disgrace. The wall of Jerusalem is broken down, and its gates have been burned with fire' (v 3).

Nehemiah was a child of the Captivity, probably descended from the tribe of Judah (see v 2). In his book, he gives us what could be called his memoirs: his account of what happened as he ministered for the Lord at a critical time in Israel's history. The story he relays is not all about him; rather, it concerns what he was able to do – with God's help – for Jerusalem and its people.

As cupbearer to the Persian king, Nehemiah had many privileges and a certain amount of power. He was the person who guarded his master's living quarters – an important responsibility which demanded that he be a person of integrity.

We can learn much about Nehemiah's character, even from the opening verses of his book. He was frank and courageous, gracious and faithful – winning the king's trust and friendship. He also showed compassion and concern for his fellow Jews, even though they were living so far away. Most of all, especially after hearing the devastating news coming out of Jerusalem, he looked to God for guidance:

When I heard these things, I sat down and wept. For some days I mourned and fasted and prayed before the God of heaven (v 4).

Our *character* is of utmost importance. Someone wrote that character is not a single quality but a three-dimensional achievement built on the foundation of decision, direction and dedication. As we will soon see, Nehemiah made wise decisions because he received direction from the Lord, and he was dedicated to help his people because of his great faith in the Lord.

Do we daily ask God to refine our character – so we can reflect the Lord's beauty in us?

PRAYER
I am *deciding* right now, Lord, to follow your *direction* as I *dedicate* my life to you afresh!

The Greatest Force

'… let your ear be attentive and your eyes open to hear the prayer your servant is praying before you day and night for your servants, the people of Israel' (v 6).

When Nehemiah heard about all the troubles taking place in Jerusalem, his first reaction was to weep. Empathy. Then, while mourning and fasting, he prayed a prayer of confession:

'We have acted very wickedly towards you. We have not obeyed the commands, decrees and laws you gave your servant Moses' (v 7).

Prayer has been called by some 'the greatest force on earth'. Yet countless people neglect praying, feeling it is somehow irrelevant in our highly sophisticated society. No one can deny, however, that so many have been sustained by prayer when faced with extremely difficult situations. Abraham Lincoln admitted: 'I have been driven many times to my knees by the overwhelming conviction that I had nowhere else to go. My own wisdom and that of those about me seemed insufficient for the day.'

So often, prayers can become a ritual. A prayer before a meal, expressed without much thought. A prayer before bedtime, our mind wandering as we reflect upon our day. But prayer – as we all well know – can be powerful, making such a difference in people's lives. Alan Redpath, a well-known British evangelist and author, writes: 'Much of our praying is just asking God to bless some folks that are ill, and to keep us plugging along. But prayer is not merely prattle: it is warfare.'[7]

Prayer. It's the greatest force on earth. It's all *about* spiritual warfare. And so we must ask: Do we pray in anticipation of what God will do in people's lives? In *our* lives? In the life of our nation? Nehemiah prayed:

'O Lord, let your ear be attentive to the prayer of this your servant and to the prayer of your servants who delight in revering your name' (v 11).

May we all be God's servants who 'delight' in praying and giving honour to the name of the Lord!

Healthy Relationships

In the month of Nisan in the twentieth year of King Artaxerxes, when wine was brought for him, I took the wine and gave it to the king (v 1).

The years following the Second World War were labelled the Cold War as nations exchanged threats and tried to gain power. The Berlin Wall, built in August 1961 by the Communist East Berlin authorities to totally encircle West Berlin, stood for almost three decades – a powerful symbol of animosity. Then, on 9 November 1989, it was announced that German citizens could cross freely from East to West. The entire wall was demolished the following year, offering long-awaited freedom. It led to the reunion of families and the re-establishment of good friendships.

Perhaps because we have been hurt in the past, we might put up barriers. We do not have the desire, the time, to invest in healthy relationships. We think we're self-sufficient. We can figure things out on our own. *Walls.*

Nehemiah counted on the good and healthy relationship he had built with the king of Persia over many years. Because of the tight connection established between the two, trust developed. There was a mutual respect. So, when Nehemiah needed a favour he said to the king:

'May the king live for ever! … If it pleases the king and if your servant has found favour in his sight, let him send me to the city in Judah where my fathers are buried so that I can rebuild it' (vv 3, 5).

The king asked Nehemiah a few more questions, knowing he would be losing a good worker and faithful friend. But since there was a healthy relationship established with the king, and because God was with Nehemiah, permission was granted for Nehemiah to leave.

What about us? Do we need to set aside time for building relationships with others? It might involve visiting them; sharing with them from the heart; supporting one another in prayer. Let's break down any walls that might hinder us. And let us also make sure we consistently strive to deepen the health of our relationship with the Lord. After all, what a *friend* we have in Jesus!

The Way, Truth, Life

Jesus answered, 'I am the way and the truth and the life. No-one comes to the Father except through me' (v 6).

Jesus, in preparation for his departure from the world – in his physical state – told his disciples to trust in him. For he was going 'to prepare a place' for them (v 2), and one day he would return to take them with him. He then said to the Twelve:

> *'You know the way to the place where I am going' (v 4).*

This baffled them. But Thomas was bold enough to say that they *did not* know where he was going. So how could they possibly know the way? A few verses earlier, we read that Peter also asked the question: 'Lord, where are you going?' (13:36). Jesus responded to both disciples with our key verse for today – telling them that *he* was, and is, the way, the truth, the life. He was leaving so he could prepare a place for them in his Father's house. Heaven. The place where God dwells; where Jesus now sits at his Father's right hand.

He prepares this place for us also! But how do we get there? The only *way*, we are told, is by acknowledging and accepting Jesus as Lord and Saviour. Not by doing good works, nor by giving costly gifts or donations, nor by observing religious ceremonies. Jesus is the one and only way for us to receive eternal life.

For he is the *truth*. All he says in the Bible is truth; all his promises given are true. And Jesus is all about *life*. Yes, the giver of eternal life, and also the giver of life for today and for tomorrow. His assurance of a heavenly home at the end of life's journey can get us through any obstacles or burdens we are facing right now: our battles or suffering. But also, he gives life purpose and meaning *now*.

Are we following the *way* of the Lord? Do we claim him as Lord of all *truth*? Are we living an abundant *life* in him?

PRAYER
Lord, you are my reason for living. Help me to reach out to others, telling them of the way, the truth, the life that can be found in *you*!

Another Counsellor

'And I will ask the Father, and he will give you another Counsellor' (v 16).

Many newspapers and magazines contain a column where people can write in to a 'counsellor', stating the various concerns going on in their lives. They usually sign with an anonymous name, like 'Confused in Canada' or 'Bewildered in Botswana' or 'Stumped in Singapore'. The person responsible for giving answers to the different problems usually tries to get right to the point of each dilemma.

Yet secular responses, although sometimes helpful, can only reach someone to a limited degree. When it comes to the heart, soul and spirit, there is only *One* who is able to give perfect answers, perfect solutions, to the questions and struggles of everyday life – having an *everlasting* significance.

Isaiah prophesied of a 'Wonderful Counsellor' to come (9:6). One who would change peoples' lives for ever. Jesus did come, and lived among his people. The time came, however, when he had to return to his Father. Yet he promised his disciples – *all* his followers – that 'another Counsellor' would come in his place:

'… to be with you for ever' (v 16).

We live in a confusing and complex world that is often fragile and frightening. Sometimes we do not know which way to turn for guidance, direction; where to go for help. Jesus urges us to bring our deepest concerns to our Counsellor. If we do, his presence in our lives will assure us that we will never be the same again!

Dear Jesus: Will you be my Counsellor, and be with me through all my problems and pain – now and always? – *'Seeking'*

Dear 'Seeking': *'Ask and it will be given to you; seek and you will find; knock and the door will be opened to you … Come to me … and I will give you rest' (Matthew 7:7; 11:28)* – **Jesus**

Inner Conflict

For I envied the arrogant when I saw the prosperity of the wicked (v 3).

The theme of this 'psalm of Asaph' is the disparity between the wicked and the good. The former often seem to win, while the latter suffer greatly. Yet do those who are evil *really* win? This is what the psalmist is struggling with; there's an inner conflict going on. Where is God when evil seems to reign? Doubts begin to fester. And if we are like Asaph, we may begin to stumble:

> *But as for me, my feet had almost slipped; I had nearly lost my foothold (v 2).*

We see those who cause others harm prosper. They seemingly have no struggles, and are healthy and strong (v 4). No burdens; no problems (v 5). They are full of such arrogant pride (v 6). Their violent acts cause so much grief, and there's no limit to their cruelty (vv 6-7). Inside we struggle with it all, asking 'Why?'

Every day we read in newspapers and hear on newscasts of such violent acts inflicted upon innocent people, including children. We are filled with rage, sickened by it all. So many culprits seem to get away with their acts of evil on a daily basis. And it has been going on like this for thousands of years.

Again, like Asaph, we cannot begin to understand all this oppressiveness, pain and tragedy. As he cries out concerning all of this, God reveals insight to the psalmist – and to us:

> *… I entered the sanctuary of God; then I understood their final destiny (v 17).*

God *will* bring justice. He understands what we are going through. All he asks is that we trust him and stay close to him, always:

> *… it is good to be near God. I have made the Sovereign LORD my refuge (v 28).*

Do we trust God – for *all* things? May it be so!

The Splendour of the King

'The wolf and the lamb will feed together, and the lion will eat straw like the ox, but dust will be the serpent's food. They will neither harm nor destroy on all my holy mountain,' says the LORD *(v 25).*

Some of the contemporary worship songs – especially those included in the new Salvation Army song book – are wonderful! The words reach down to the depth of our soul. Today's song speaks of our majestic Lord Jesus, in all his 'splendour' and 'majesty'. The whole earth rejoicing, even *trembling*, in awe of his voice. Why? Because our God is so awesome:

> The splendour of the King, clothed in majesty;
> Let all the earth rejoice …
>> How great, how great is our God.
>>> (*SASB* 64 v 1, refrain)

Chris Tomlin, along with Jesse Reeves and Ed Cash, released this song in 2004. It became one of the top worship songs, mainly because it is theologically sound. Also, because it speaks of a day when there will be peace on earth – the lion, the lamb, living together in harmony; a day when good will triumph over evil. Hallelujah!

How we need to hear these words of hope and assurance in these days of constant turmoil and upheaval. Yes, indeed, our God *is* great – and so worthy of our praise! So, let us conclude our worship time today by pondering on the closing words of this powerful song. They remind us of the wonderful name of Jesus and of our great God:

> Name above all names, worthy of all praise;
> My heart will sing: how great is our God.[8]

PRAYER
Father, we pay homage to the name and authority of Jesus. May we sing praises to him – all to the glory of our great God.

Three Days

I went to Jerusalem, and after staying there three days … I said to them … 'Come, let us rebuild' (vv 11, 17).

After Nehemiah made the journey from Susa to Jerusalem, he took three days to just be still. Three days to assess the situation at hand. Three days to observe how everyone was working – or not working – as it related to the rebuilding of the city. Three days, perhaps for purification purposes; but for certain, to wait on the Lord – seeking wisdom and guidance for what lay ahead. To prepare his body, mind, soul and spirit.

We live in an 'instant' society. We receive an email and feel the urgent need to respond. When a text appears on our phone, it calls out to us for an immediate answer. But so often it is wise to just wait; to pause, think things through and pray things through before answering – so we will have no regrets in reacting impulsively.

After the three days of praying and seeking the Lord's direction, Nehemiah went about Jerusalem seeing exactly what needed to be done in order to move forward. He then called his people together, challenging and encouraging *all* of them to work together – to get involved – because God would be their guide. Their response?

'Let us start rebuilding' (v 18).

Outsiders mocked them as they began to work. Nehemiah replied:

'The God of heaven will give us success' (v 20).

Whether we are facing a difficult situation at work, or within the context of our family, or even something quite personal, let's make sure we always take time – a day, even *three* days or more – to pray about it and sense God's guidance. It will never, ever, be time wasted!

Prayer
Help me to be patient, Lord, and to *always* make time for you to reveal your will for my life.

Adversity

When Sanballat heard that we were rebuilding the wall, he became angry and was greatly incensed. He ridiculed the Jews … 'What are those feeble Jews doing?' (vv 1-2).

In chapter 3 of Nehemiah we are told that the wall of Jerusalem was being built. In this next chapter, and those immediately following, we discover *how* it was being built – and the adversity the Jews faced. The opening verse tells us that Sanballat, the Samaritan, was full of anger at what was happening – ridiculing the Jews and calling them 'feeble'. His friend, Tobiah, joined in:

'What they are building – if even a fox climbed up on it, he would break down their wall of stones!' (v 3).

Sarah Young, an American-born missionary, writes this – as if from God's perspective: 'Expect to encounter adversity in your life, remembering that you live in a deeply fallen world. Stop trying to find a way that circumvents difficulties. The main problem with an easy life is that it masks your need for Me. When you became a Christian, I infused My very Life into you, empowering you to live on a supernatural plane by depending on Me. Anticipate coming face-to-face with impossibilities: situations totally beyond your ability to handle … When you see armies of problems marching toward you, cry out to Me! Allow Me to fight for you. Watch Me working on your behalf, as you rest in the shadow of My Almighty Presence.'[9]

Sometimes we are simply baffled, wondering why there is adversity in our lives. We regret how it affects us, playing into every aspect of what we strive to do. Nehemiah knew these external insults were greatly discouraging his people, so called out to God for help. He knew that when we face affliction, only God can bring any sense of peace – giving us resolve and strength to move forward:

So we rebuilt the wall till all of it reached half its height, for the people worked with all their heart (v 6).

Lessons Learned

But when Sanballat, Tobiah, the Arabs, the Ammonites and the men of Ashdod heard that the repairs to Jerusalem's walls had gone ahead and that the gaps were being closed, they were very angry. They all plotted together to come and fight against Jerusalem and stir up trouble against it (vv 7-8).

Nehemiah and his people got through the taunts of Sanballat, finishing half of the wall. But when others joined in on the harassing and the hardships continued, the people soon became discouraged. Then, when they saw the enemy coming to fight, they were suddenly gripped by fear. Nehemiah's response?

But we prayed to our God and posted a guard day and night to meet this threat (v 9).

Can lessons be learned from facing adversity? Of course, even though no one wishes to go through hard times. Learning to handle difficult situations – without losing our emotional balance – takes patience, and great spiritual maturity. Here are a few possible lessons:

Lesson 1. Pray. When facing any kind of conflict or suffering, we are to bring the situation to God in prayer. To seek his direction, his wisdom. It must always be our first priority.

Lesson 2. Guard our hearts. In Nehemiah's case, they put a guard on watch, day and night. We must always protect what is important to us, preventing the enemy from taking over.

Lesson 3. Include others. Share what we are going through with trusted friends – so prayer can be offered. Before, Nehemiah had always prayed *for* his people. Now he prayed *with* his people: 'But we prayed to our God' (v 9).

Lesson 4. Acknowledge God's presence. Even though the people were experiencing great fear and anxiety, thinking they were doomed, Nehemiah reminded them – and *us* – that God is always with us, for us, and will see through *all* that lies ahead:

'Don't be afraid of them. Remember the Lord, who is great and awesome' (v 14).

Belonging to Jesus

And you also are among those who are called to belong to Jesus Christ (v 6).

Romans may be the most important letter we will ever read. When Augustine read it in the late 4th century, it greatly helped take away doubts that were lingering in his heart. Centuries later, John Calvin said that reading Romans would help open minds to understanding *all* Scripture. It dramatically changed the life of Martin Luther, causing him to nail his 95 Theses on the Castle Church in Wittenberg, Germany – the beginning of the Protestant Reformation. And for John Wesley, Romans was transformational – helping to launch the great 18th-century evangelical revival in England.

Romans is also important for us today! For Scripture is:

… the power of God for the salvation of everyone who believes (v 16).

Although Paul did not found the church in Rome, he knew Christians who were there. He wanted them to be strengthened in their faith; to really know what salvation is all about. Being Paul's greatest theological work, this letter is sometimes difficult to grasp. But it is fascinating to read, and is meant to encourage us in our faith and our spiritual walk with the Lord. After all, it reminds us we are declared *righteous* through our faith in Christ (Romans 5:1; Galatians 2:16).

Right at the beginning of the letter Paul tells the Christians in Rome – and he tells us – that we are called to 'belong to Jesus Christ'. Beautiful words! But *do* we feel called to belong to the Lord? Called to live for him; sacrifice for him. Called to be joined with Christ; willing to forsake the things of this world that may appear exciting, may even be enticing – all because of this sense of belonging. If the answer is 'yes', then Romans is for us: to empower, strengthen and encourage us. And as God's righteous people, we are to live, day by day, by *faith* in him:

'The righteous will live by faith' (v 17).

Prayer
Increase my faith, O Lord. And may your precious Holy Spirit help me to be your faithful, righteous servant.

God's Wrath and Righteousness

They exchanged the truth of God for a lie, and worshipped and served created things rather than the Creator – who is for ever praised. Amen (1:25).

God hates sin. We, on the other hand, often toy with it – worshipping other 'things' rather than God himself. When we do this, we are virtually telling God he is not worthy of our praise. Our love for him is less than our longing to fulfil our selfish desires.

Paul tells us that it is not just about the sin itself, but what's going on inside us. For when we choose to sin, we are suppressing the truth about God: who he is, and what he means to us personally. If we love God, why do we so often turn our backs on him?

When we engage in wickedness, in sin, Creator God must respond:

The wrath of God is being revealed from heaven against all the godlessness and wickedness of men who suppress the truth by their wickedness (1:18).

We don't like to talk about God's wrath. Yet sin is serious business! We deserve to be punished. Paul tells us, however, that there is good news. God is *righteous*, and he will forgive and even smile upon us – but only if we are repentant, striving not to sin again:

To those who by persistence in doing good seek glory, honour and immortality, he will give eternal life (2:7).

It's up to us. We can treat sin lightly or we can ask the Holy Spirit to cleanse us, helping us to focus only on Christ. Then there will be:

… glory, honour and peace for everyone who does good (2:10).

PRAYER
Father, I don't like to read about your wrath; yet it makes me more acutely aware of my sin and its ugliness. Help me, by your Holy Spirit, to be more and more like Jesus.

Things of the Heart

To man belong the plans of the heart, but from the LORD *comes the reply of the tongue. All a man's ways seem innocent to him, but motives are weighed by the* LORD *(vv 1-2).*

When we speak about things of the heart, it gets very personal. What is going on in our heart? Good things? Not-so-great things? What things do we *plan* in our heart? And what's the *motive* behind what we do? Solomon addresses 'heart' issues here in Proverbs 16. He refers to several things that can hold us back, but then moves on to good things that bring us closer to the Lord.

A deceitful heart. Right at the beginning, we are presented with the notion of motive. If we do good things, but with wrong motive, we are being deceitful. If we say nice things, but don't mean what we say, we are being deceitful. Others might not get it right away; but the Lord knows – for he sees our heart.

A proud heart. No one likes people who are full of pride and self-glory. Especially the Lord. In fact, he 'detests' this kind of heart:

The LORD *detests all the proud of heart (v 5).*

Rather than hearts full of deceit, or pride, we can have hearts that are turned toward God and his ways.

A discerning heart. When we call on the Lord for every step we take in life, God is pleased with us – for we become a discerning people:

The wise in heart are called discerning (v 21).

A wise heart. When we daily call upon the Lord's wisdom, we speak good and pleasant words that bring help to others:

A wise man's heart guides his mouth … Pleasant words are a honeycomb, sweet to the soul and healing to the bones (vv 23-24).

PRAYER

When it comes to things of the heart, make me more like you, Jesus; give me a heart that's filled with love!

Tell Me the Stories

… he explained to them what was said in all the Scriptures concerning himself (v 27).

Most people love a good story! Especially children. My little grandchildren love it when I sit them on my knee and read a story to them, or simply tell them one. And when it's a story about Jesus, they seem fascinated!

> Tell me the stories of Jesus I love to hear;
> Things I would ask him to tell me If he were here:
> Scenes by the wayside, Tales of the sea,
> Stories of Jesus, Tell them to me.   (*SASB* 151 v 1)

It is important that we commence telling stories of Jesus in the home. Then, it's important to make it our mission to tell these same stories in our Sunday schools. Young people need to know that Jesus blessed the children, and still longs to bless them today:

> First let me hear how the children Stood round his knee;
> And I shall fancy his blessing Resting on me;
> Words full of kindness, Deeds full of grace,
> All in the love-light Of Jesus' face.   (v 2)

William H. Parker, an English Baptist layman who was very much interested in the work of Sunday schools, wrote these lyrics in the early 1900s after a child in his class said, 'Teacher, tell us another story.' Adults *also* love to hear stories of Jesus: his birth, life, death, resurrection, ascension – knowing he is one day coming back, so we can be with him for ever! Let's sing, or read, this final verse while thinking of one person with whom we can share stories of Jesus this week:

> Show me that scene, in the garden, Of bitter pain;
> And of the cross where my Saviour For me was slain;
> Sad ones or bright ones, So that they be
> Stories of Jesus; Tell them to me.

Becoming as One

Now the men and their wives raised a great outcry against their Jewish brothers (v 1).

There were bursts of anger from the people. Why? Because the rich were getting richer and the poor poorer. Sounds familiar? It's been forever thus. In this case, 90 years earlier, the first group of exiles returning from Babylon to Jerusalem brought worldly goods, given to them by fellow Jews (see Ezra 1:5-6). Even King Cyrus lavished them with gold and silver (Ezra 1:7-11). When they finally arrived in Jerusalem, they built panelled homes (see Haggai 1:4). They were wealthy!

When the second group of exiles returned, they also were lavished with gifts from their wealthy relatives who stayed back in Babylon (see Zechariah 6:10-11). But the Jews who had always remained in Jerusalem were *not* well off at all. Our Scripture for today tells us the merchants and labourers had no income. The farmers had to mortgage their fields, vineyards and homes in order to buy grain to feed their families. Also, they were required to pay taxes, so had to borrow money – a further burden placed upon them.

Nehemiah was angry because those who *did* have much financially were now exploiting those who had so little. He gathered the people together, challenging the wealthy to restore land to their fellow Jews, and to lend them money and grain without interest:

'Give back to them immediately their fields, vineyards … also the usury you are charging them' (v 11).

They listened to Nehemiah, and answered:

'We will give it back' (v 12).

The assembly praised the Lord *together* – becoming as one. As a unified body of those who loved God, they then said: 'Amen' (v 13).

PRAYER
Lord, help me to *give* from the heart; to become as one with my brothers and sisters around the world – and in my own community.

Keeping our Cool

'Moreover, according to these reports you are about to become their king and have even appointed prophets to make this proclamation about you in Jerusalem: "There is a king in Judah!"' (vv 6-7).

Have you ever been falsely accused of doing or saying something? Your character attacked or questioned? We are not sure how to respond, and sometimes we find it hard keeping our cool.

Sanballat and Geshem were taunting Nehemiah, pretending they wanted to meet with him as friends. But the truth finally came out, by way of an unsealed letter. The men were accusing Nehemiah of plotting to revolt against those outside Jerusalem. This was the real reason for rebuilding the city's wall. Nehemiah would soon declare himself to be king, having people praise him.

But Nehemiah saw through these men, knowing they were trying to intimidate him and tear down his character; trying to frighten him and make him vulnerable – so they could attack Nehemiah's people. Nehemiah sent back his reply with the messenger:

'Nothing like what you are saying is happening' (v 8).

When our character is attacked, our motives are questioned, when we're falsely accused, first we must take a deep breath – rather than immediately retaliate. Then we must bring it all before the Lord, seeking wisdom in how to respond appropriately. If we truly feel we have done nothing wrong, we must declare our innocence in a way that is pleasing to God. Keeping our cool.

Finally, as Nehemiah did, we are to ask God to strengthen us for whatever task lies ahead:

But I prayed, 'Now strengthen my hands' (v 9).

Then the 'wall' – the particular task God has for us – *will* be accomplished:

So the wall was completed (v 15).

PRAYER
Help me to always keep my cool, Lord – even when attacked – so I can be effective in my service for you.

Accomplishment

When all our enemies heard about this, all the surrounding nations were afraid and lost their self-confidence, because they realised that this work had been done with the help of our God (6:16).

The Jerusalem wall was completed. What an accomplishment! Everyone had dug in and got involved. The rich, the poor; those who had always been in Jerusalem, and the returned exiles. The Jewish nation felt good. The men and women, as well as the children, were now protected; everyone felt strong and confident. And best of all, the people knew this accomplishment had only been possible because the Lord was *with* them, his very own people.

Nehemiah put in place his brother Hanani to be in charge of Jerusalem, along with Hananiah as commander – a man who greatly loved the Lord. Gatekeepers were appointed as guards during the day, but the people themselves were to guard the wall at night:

> *'Also appoint residents of Jerusalem as guards, some at their posts and some near their own houses' (7:3).*

Yes, *everyone* was responsible for guarding what they had accomplished together. It was a team effort. They all got involved in protecting what was theirs. For Jerusalem represented God's presence with his people.

If someone were to ask you to state your five top accomplishments so far in life, what would they be? If you can, jot them down on a piece of paper, right now. After doing this, ask yourself how many of these needed God's assistance. It is important to remember that only things we accomplish with God's help have eternal value.

Whether it's a wall built, a well-delivered sermon, or the raising of a child, let's make sure *all* we strive to accomplish in life is credited to the Lord. Shall we give praise and glory to him – right now?

PONDER

Not in my own strength can I accomplish
All thou art planning for me , day by day
(Jessie Caroline Mountain, *SASB* 599 v 3)

Big Me

There is no difference, for all have sinned and fall short of the glory of God (vv 22-23).

In the movie *The Fellowship of the Ring* – based on the first volume of J.R.R. Tolkien's classic novel *The Lord of the Rings* – Frodo the Hobbit says: 'I wish none of this had happened.' Gandalf, his mentor and friend, replies: 'So do all who live to see such times, but that is not for them to decide. All we have to decide is what to do with the time that is given to us.' The gift of choice. We have no choice in *when* we live; we do have a choice in *how* we are to live.

In today's Scripture, Paul reminds us that we all have sinned. Fallen from experiencing fellowship with God. All because of sin. But – as we were reminded yesterday – there is good news. When we repent, turning our eyes upon Jesus, we are:

… justified freely by his grace (v 24).

Forgiven! Justified. As if we had never sinned. All because of God's *amazing grace*. Sometimes we forget how sinful we truly are, right at the core of our being. Perhaps we need a reality check – stark as it may be. What we really deserve is hell! *But*, because of God's grace, Christ's sacrifice on the Cross for you and for me, we will live with him for ever in Heaven. *Grace.* How sweet the sound! So, what *will* we do with the rest of the time given to us?

We close with excerpts from a prayer-poem which asks God to deliver us from *self*, from sin – enabling us to embrace God's love and his beautiful grace:

Today, Lord, has been a bad day. Big Me obscured my vision.
Not only my vision of other people and their interests, that would
        have been bad enough, but worse, Master.
Big Me obscured my vision of you …
I sat in a sacred service. One of your servants was proclaiming the
        rich mercies of your grace; I only heard Big Me's complaints …
Tender verses from your book were read; Big Me was unmoved.
What can I do, Master, when Big Me takes the reins?
Can you deliver me from his dominance?[10]

Peace with God

Therefore, since we have been justified through faith, we have peace with God through our Lord Jesus Christ (v 1).

Peace with God.
Nothing quite like it!
Knowing we need not have any fear, because of our past;
no penalty, on God's part, because
Christ paid the price on the Cross for us.
Because we have this peace, deep within, we long to share it with others.
Yet so easily we get caught up in the perpetual treadmill of life.
Stress. Anxiety. Pressure.
How can we outwardly express this peace?

By holding a baby.
Stooping to smell flowers along the garden path.
Listening to the birds singing their melodious tunes.
Admiring the myriad of colours in a distant rainbow.
Being still …

We all long for peace in our world.
We begin by extending the hand of friendship to another.
Helping a neighbour in need.
Being by someone's side; simply listening to their story.
Sharing *our* story of transformation.

We come before God in humbleness of spirit.
To pray. To commune. To fellowship.
Sealing our commitment, our consecration.
O, how we love you, Saviour!

Peace … with God … through our Lord Jesus Christ.

Perfect peace!

God's Wonderful Deeds

*We give thanks to you, O God, we give thanks, for your Name is near;
men tell of your wonderful deeds (75:1).*

Several years ago I read of a heroic story coming from Kanpur, India. The
title of the report in the newspaper read: 'Hero monkey performs CPR on
friend'. Immediately catching my attention, I read on. An injured monkey
had fallen between some railroad tracks after touching high-tension electric
wires. He lay on his back, rigid and lifeless. His companion came to the
rescue by lifting up the motionless body, shaking it, then teething his friend's
neck and scalp. Slowly, the monkey came back to life.

If we can read of a monkey coming to the aid of his friend, and be awed
by it, how much more should we *marvel* at all God does for us! Daily, the
Lord works out salvation for us – being there for us, and helping us through
all our difficulties and trials:

*But you, O God, are my king from of old; you bring salvation upon the
earth (74:12).*

God brings each one of us abundant life. He protects and defends us; he
looks out for us and watches over us – for he is Creator God, and we are his
creation:

*It was you who set all the boundaries of the earth; you made both summer
and winter (v 17).*

We instinctively want to 'give thanks' to God, for all his wonderful deeds
on our behalf. For guiding, directing, caring, rescuing. And because he *loves*
us so greatly, we can *trust* him supremely – telling others of his wonderful,
awesome, marvellous deeds:

*As for me, I will declare this for ever; I will sing praise to the God of Jacob
(75:9).*

Prayer
**Thank you, Creator God, for *all* you have done, are doing, and will do for
me. I love you – with all my heart!**

I'm Set Apart for Jesus

And he said unto them, Come ye yourselves apart into a desert place, and rest a while (v 31 KJV).

To be 'set apart' for Jesus does not mean we need to necessarily get away from everyone else, but it does mean we are to take time to 'rest' in the Lord. Being 'set apart' doesn't mean we're better than anyone else, but it does mean we are clothed in God's holiness, resisting all evil, and fully consecrated to him:

> I'm set apart for Jesus, To be a king and priest;
> His life in me increases, Upon his love I feast.
> From evil separated, Made holy by his blood,
> My all is consecrated Unto the living God. (*SASB* 255 v 1)

Why do we choose to be set apart for the Lord? Because we see in him his 'goodness' and because he promises to keep us 'clean' within. We become *one* with him – in our actions, speech, thought-life. God empowers us daily to be more and more like his Son:

> I'm set apart for Jesus, His goodness I have seen,
> He makes my heart his altar, He keeps his temple clean.
> Our union none can sever, Together every hour,
> His life is mine for ever With resurrection power. (v 2)

William James Pearson, the songwriter, joined The Christian Mission in 1874 and was stationed in Bradford in 1878, when the Mission became known as The Salvation Army. He often wrote a new song every week. The final verse of today's song reminds us that *all* foes can be driven away when we call on God's strength. With him, we *can* overcome the world:

> I'm set apart for Jesus, With him to ever stay,
> My spirit he releases, He drives my foes away.
> He gives full strength for trial And shields when darts are hurled;
> With him and self-denial I overcome the world.

Let's declare our obedience to the Lord, now and for always!

Revival Meeting

They told Ezra the scribe to bring out the Book of the Law of Moses, which the LORD had commanded for Israel (v 1).

Although a census had been taken of all the Israelite families and their genealogies (chapter 7), the men and women came to the realisation that they needed to get right with God in order to move forward. So they gathered together, asking Ezra to read to them from God's Word – as well as to pray for them:

Ezra praised the LORD, the great God; and all the people lifted their hands and responded, 'Amen! Amen!' Then they bowed down and worshipped the LORD with their faces to the ground (v 6).

A revival meeting! Their hearts were being prepared to hear from God, and there was great anticipation and excitement in the air. As they listened to the Word being read – 'from daybreak till noon' (v 3) – they actually *wept* (v 9). But there was also joy and celebration:

'Go and enjoy choice food and sweet drinks … for the joy of the LORD is your strength' … Then all the people went away … to celebrate with great joy (vv 10, 12).

Have you been part of a revival? Perhaps a service when many people accepted Christ as Saviour or rededicated their lives to him. There's nothing quite like it! It might take place in a huge congress meeting or rally; or it could happen in our own corps or church – even a few in our own home. Wherever it takes place, there *is* usually weeping; but there's celebration too – as it was with the Israelites:

Day after day, from the first day to the last, Ezra read from the Book of the Law of God. They celebrated (v 18).

Let's pause and *celebrate* God right now – wherever we find ourselves. Do you sense a stirring in your soul? If so, share 'the joy of the Lord' with someone today. Maybe you will have your own revival meeting!

Signing our Name on the Line

'In view of all this, we are making a binding agreement, putting it in writing, and our leaders, our Levites and our priests are affixing their seals to it' (9:38).

The people of Judah had suddenly become hungry for the Word, God's Law, to be read to them. There was a revival, a renewal, as they bowed before Almighty God. They wept, but were also filled with a deep joy. This was all in preparation for the 'binding agreement' they were to make as God's covenanted people.

We are given a record of those who signed their names on the line (see 10:1-27), those who affixed their seals to the covenant made with God. This indicated they were in total agreement in keeping their commitment to the Lord.

When I was in university – many years ago now – I was not always living according to God's standard. With time, I realised the life I was experiencing wasn't for me. One Sunday I gave my life to Christ, in total commitment. I recall my dad – Clarence Burrows, a Salvation Army officer – saying to me, 'Have you really signed your name on the line?' In other words, is this truly a *full* commitment to the Lord? I humbly responded that it was – and testify that it still is today!

The leaders in Nehemiah's day did likewise, giving themselves fully to God: a total commitment – setting an example for many others to follow.

When I changed my lifestyle at university, many of my friends were quite shocked and questioned why I was committing myself to God in this way. It caused some to look at their own lives – how *they* were living. We are to be examples for others; never to think ourselves as better than others in any way, but only doing what God requires us to do.

Nehemiah signed his name on the line. Others followed. Do we need to sign our names – or *re-sign* them – sealing our commitment to God?

PRAYER

Father, in my heart right now I want to seal and renew my covenant – because I love you with all I have and all that I am!

Time to Party!

At the dedication of the wall of Jerusalem, the Levites were sought out from where they lived and were brought to Jerusalem to celebrate joyfully the dedication with songs of thanksgiving and with the music of cymbals, harps and lyres (12:27).

Everyone loves a good party! Whether it's a birthday celebration or a special occasion of another nature, when we are invited to a party we anticipate lots of good music, food, fun and laughter. People come with smiles on their faces and joy in their hearts.

With the completion of the wall of Jerusalem, it was time to dedicate it to the Lord – in the form of a great party! Everyone was invited, for they had accomplished this task *together*. After sealing their covenant with God, it was now time to celebrate.

Nehemiah assigned different people to different activities for this great celebration. Some played cymbals, harps and lyres. Others sang or played various instruments:

> *I also assigned two large choirs to give thanks … as well as some priests with trumpets … with musical instruments prescribed by David the man of God (31, 35, 36).*

Quite the party! But in all of this, Nehemiah did not want the people to ever forget the significance of all that had taken place. In the final chapter of his book, several times he says to God 'remember me' or 'remember them' – for God to remember his people and for the people to remember and honour the Lord, *always*. Nehemiah wanted *all* that had transpired to be consecrated to the Lord.

The Christian life is to be one of dedication and commitment. But it's also to be filled with great joy and celebration. At the end of the day, even after we 'party' because of our deep love for God, may we forever prove to be people of highest integrity; people who are faithful to the Lord. And as we sense God smiling upon us, let's say with Nehemiah, in humble consecration:

> *Remember me with favour, O my God (13:31).*

Sin is No Joke

For the wages of sin is death, but the gift of God is eternal life in Christ Jesus our Lord (v 23).

Many fear death. The loss of a loved one. The dread of one's own life coming to an end – and what may come before it: suffering; pain; possible loss of memory or dignity. But when we speak of *spiritual* death, there is much more to fear. For this kind of death results in the loss of hope, the loss of eternal life.

Why would people, even Christians, then *choose* to sin – knowing that 'the wages of sin is death'? Why risk the chance of not being able to live with Christ eternally? Paul wanted to address this very issue because he knew it was vital for Christians to grasp; to comprehend the consequences of sin.

Somehow they were under the assumption that the more they sinned, the more grace would be given to them:

Shall we go on sinning, so that grace may increase? By no means! We died to sin; how can we live in it any longer? (vv 1-2).

Paul includes himself, by using the word 'we', for he was tempted to sin just like everyone else. But sin is no joke. Not to be toyed with, ever. So Paul gives some strong and serious counsel:

… count yourselves dead to sin but alive to God in Christ Jesus (v 11).

Paul assures the Christians in Rome – just as he assures us – that, by the help of the Holy Spirit, we are released from our slavery to sin when Jesus becomes Lord of our lives. And the best news of all: when we embrace the truth of being now dead to sin, and its hold on us, we then receive the gift of eternal life!

PRAYER
Lord God, make me enslaved to *you*, I pray!

Shame

But in order that sin might be recognised as sin, it produced death in me through what was good, so that through the commandment sin might become utterly sinful (v 13).

Have you ever experienced shame? Most of us can identify with it. Sadly, shame can linger – if not dealt with properly. And if we have never felt shame, we know nothing of God's holiness.

Children often exhibit shame, especially when it comes to disappointing their parents. Teenagers feel shame when they've experimented with something they knew was not right – not of God. Adults experience shame when they've greatly let someone down – especially someone they love.

Paul makes his comments very personal when writing to the Christians in Rome about sin and shame:

I do not understand what I do. For what I want to do I do not do, but what I hate I do … As it is, it is no longer I myself who do it, but it is sin living in me (vv 15, 17).

There's no excuse. No one, no *thing*, to blame – other than ourselves when we mess up. And this brings shame. Why? Because:

… in my inner being I delight in God's law (v 22).

We *know* what's right and what's wrong. After all, we 'delight' in God's law and want to please him! Yet … we consistently let God down – which results in shame. And we feel horrible!

But we can *rid* ourselves of this shame, simply by asking forgiveness. Yes, there may be consequences on a human level. But we can be cleansed, purified, restored. The shame, gone – by God's grace and through his precious Holy Spirit.

If we are living with shame, right now, please pray with me.

PRAYER
O God, I ask your forgiveness. Make me *clean* … and may your Holy Spirit touch my life afresh, I pray.

The God of Miracles

You are the God who performs miracles (77:14).

Many people know nothing of God, so are not aware of the wonders and miracles he performs daily. They live in darkness, failing to acknowledge that it is the Lord who makes the sun rise each morning and causes it to set at night. People fail to admit that it's God who breathes into all of us the miracle of life. He feeds us, protects and guides us, loves us.

Psalm 76 reminds us, however, that God *is* known to his people:

In Judah God is known; his name is great in Israel (v 1).

Those who *know* God want to honour him, admiring his greatness:

You are resplendent with light, more majestic than mountains rich with game (v 4).

In Psalm 77 the psalmist continues to assure us that when we are troubled in spirit, the God of miracles is always available to help us. When we sing our 'songs in the night' (v 6) – sad songs, perhaps because of sickness or anxiety or pain – God hears and wants to bring comfort. He then invites us to meditate upon his Word, to remember that he is *with* us – always:

I will meditate on all your works and consider all your mighty deeds. Your ways, O God, are holy. What god is so great as our God? (vv 12-13).

There *is* no god like our God! One who performs miracles daily, just for us, because he loves us so very much. In response, let's give thanks to him, right now, as we bow before him in prayer.

PRAYER
Loving and holy God – God of miracles and God of love, thank you for loving *me* with an everlasting love!

Jesus, Tender Lover

May God himself … make you holy and whole, put you together –
spirit, soul, and body – and keep you fit for the coming of our Master,
Jesus Christ (v 23 MSG).

It is wonderful to come before the Lord in prayer, telling him how much
we love him, confessing that he means *everything* to us!

> Jesus, tender lover of my soul,
> Pardoner of my sins, and friend indeed,
> Keeper of the garden of my heart,
> Jesus, thou art everything to me.   (*SASB* 502 v 1)

The refrain of this song was written first, by Arthur S. Arnott. He had
become a Salvation Army officer in 1898. When Edward Joy heard the
chorus used in a congress meeting in Melbourne, Australia, he wrote verses
to go with it. The second verse speaks about joys we experience, the sights
we see; yet nothing compares with seeing Jesus:

> What to me are all the joys of earth?
> What to me is every sight I see,
> Save the sight of thee, O friend of mine?
> Jesus, thou art everything to me.

The final verse reminds us of the Cross and how we must realise daily
what Christ has done – and continues to do – for us:

> Here I lay me at thy bleeding feet,
> Deepest homage now I give to thee;
> Hear thy whispered love within my soul;
> Jesus, thou art everything to me.

Is Jesus everything to us? Are *all* our lasting joys found in him? If so,
sing the refrain with me – as we think only of Christ right now:

> Jesus, thou art everything to me, Jesus, thou art everything to me,
> All my lasting joys are found in thee; Jesus, thou art everything to me.

Is Life just all Smoke?

These are the words of the Quester, David's son and king in Jerusalem: Smoke, nothing but smoke … There's nothing to anything – it's all smoke (vv 1-2 MSG).

Solomon, a king of worldwide acclaim, had it all! Wealth, fame, success. But he spent a lot of time thinking about life and its meaning. His philosophical thoughts are recorded for us in this book of Ecclesiastes. His initial thoughts are that life is really just smoke. Empty. Meaningless. Futile. How depressing!

Yet could it be that some people think along these lines? That there is no purpose for our existence? After all, the 'Quester' writes:

One generation goes its way, the next one arrives, but nothing changes – it's business as usual for old planet earth. The sun comes up and the sun goes down, then does it again, and again … The wind blows south, the wind blows north. Around and around and around it blows (vv 4-6 MSG).

Ceaseless cycles. A merry-go-round with seemingly no music in the background. Pointless. Going nowhere.

Some people *have* lost purpose, concluding that they merely exist for no real reason. Then, when things come crashing down on them, when everything goes wrong, when they experience suffering and pain, when all seems lost – they have nowhere to turn. How sad this is. Yet it's seemingly a reality for many people.

As we look at this unique and challenging book, may our hearts be open to all God has to say to us.

Action
Let's try to meet up with someone today – perhaps over coffee or tea, or simply by phone. Pose the question: 'What do *you* think life is all about?' Then let them know you believe God is sovereign and *does* have a plan and purpose for us all. If appropriate, ask if you could close your time together with prayer. It could be the beginning of further conversations in days to come!

Entitlement

I denied myself nothing my eyes desired; I refused my heart no pleasure (v 10).

There seems to be a culture of 'entitlement' that exists today. People, and even young people, feel they *deserve* certain things, that what they *desire* should be theirs. If I want, I get! This whole notion of entitlement breeds greed, envy, selfishness. And it's not healthy – in any way.

Nothing new! Solomon felt he should have anything he longed for. Even entitled to have 700 wives and 300 concubines (see 1 Kings 11:3). Today's reading says he denied himself nothing – that he 'refused no pleasure'. What he wanted, he got! This general philosophy behind 'entitlement' has an extremely negative impact on not only the people themselves, but also on society as a whole.

The Teacher, engaged in the pleasures of life, also finds work like 'a chasing after the wind' (v 17). He feels he's entitled to sit back and do nothing, because his work and toil are 'meaningless and a great misfortune' (v 21). No fulfilment. No joy found in employment of any kind. Emptiness. How depressing!

Yet Solomon, a deep thinker, soon comes to the realisation that there possibly *is* something more to life 'under the sun' (v 18). Something that has meaning; something of the eternal:

> *A man can do nothing better than to eat and drink and find satisfaction in his work. This too, I see, is from the hand of God, for without him, who can eat or find enjoyment? To the man who pleases him, God gives wisdom, knowledge and happiness … (vv 24-25).*

May we never adopt the concept – the culture – of entitlement. Rather, let us open our eyes to see God for who he is. Then, let's *worship* him – for he, alone, is entitled to be praised and honoured!

Prayer
Lord, keep me humble and forever thankful.

There is a Season

There is a time for everything, and a season for every activity under heaven (v 1).

I am not well versed when it comes to knowing much about pop music. But certain songs from over the years *do* stick out in my mind – such as 'Turn! Turn! Turn! (To Everything There Is A Season)' written by Pete Seeger and made popular by the American folk rock band The Byrds in the mid-1960s. The lyrics for the song are adapted, word for word, from the portion of Scripture we have for today.

Originally written by King Solomon, the verses in Ecclesiastes chapter 3 point out that there is a season, a time and place for all things: to be born and to die; to kill and heal; to weep and laugh; to be silent and to speak; to love and hate; for war and peace. In the 60s and moving forward, it was wonderful to hear Scripture sung over rock stations – people from a myriad of backgrounds listening to and singing Scripture. For these specific words get us thinking about what life is really all about.

Yes, there *is* a season for all things. And we must allow these 'seasons' to take place. Taking time to mourn, but also allowing ourselves to dance. Taking time to stand back, but then moving forward to embrace. Taking time to plant, but then coming to a realisation that we might have to uproot.

These are powerful and enlightening words – for all ages, for all generations. Verses that cause us to stop and think, then to ask God for direction as we move along the journey of life. It is Scripture that makes us 'turn' and, yes, even to turn again and again – to see new directions, new opportunities, God has for each one of us.

May we be open to the continual leading of his Holy Spirit as we come before him in earnest prayer.

PRAYER

Holy God, no matter what season I am experiencing right now, may I see you in it, and working through it with me. May I realise, with absolute certainty, that you are forever with me – as I anticipate *new* and *exciting* seasons of life you have in store for me!

Set Free!

Therefore, there is now no condemnation for those who are in Christ Jesus, because through Christ Jesus the law of the Spirit of life set me free (vv 1-2).

Freedom. What a beautiful word! To be set free – implying we were once bound in 'chains', but that is now no longer a reality! Oh yes, there will always be struggles in life, issues that must be dealt with and worked out. There will be temptations that lie before us. But when we give our lives fully to Christ, knowing our sins forgiven, there is a whole new dimension to life – which changes everything. There is 'no condemnation'; the binding shackles are gone. And this new freedom sets our focus on better things:

… those who live in accordance with the Spirit have their minds set on what the Spirit desires (v 5).

What *does* the Spirit desire of us? To *do* things that please God; to *be* men and women who long to honour God in every way. Since we are no longer slaves to sin, as Paul reminds us, we are *free* to live in accordance with the Holy Spirit. And if we walk in the Spirit, daily, we will have no desire to sin. It's transformational!

… those who are led by the Spirit of God are children of God… And by him we cry, 'Abba, Father' (vv 14-15 NIV2011).

Such intimacy! *'Daddy', 'Papa'.* We become his, and he is ours. Family. Fellowship. All this! And set free – to live and love. Who would want to live one more day any other way?

PRAYER
Father God – *'Daddy'* – thank you for setting me free! May I never abuse the freedom I have in you. Rather, I want to celebrate it and share this new and marvellous freedom with others. Your love, *'Papa'*, is amazing!

More than Conquerors

And we know that in all things God works for the good of those who love him, who have been called according to his purpose (v 28).

When Roman conquerors returned from war, a parade was quickly organised to honour their triumph. Trumpeters, along with other musicians; strange animals from conquered territories – often pulling carts laden with captured treasures. The general rides in a fancy chariot, basking in the celebration. But the glory is fleeting. Soon there would be another war.

Paul tells the Christians that life in Christ is not something that is here today and gone tomorrow. It is ongoing, and it is eternal! For certain, Christian living is not always easy. Trials do come to us all, and often there are many difficulties along life's journey. But God promises us that he will work all things out, according to his perfect plan. And it *will* be 'for the good' – for he loves us so deeply, so passionately.

The spiritual life is mysterious, no question; yet it is also so very wonderful – just to see how God works all things out. We can look back, seeing how the Master Weaver has put things together, enabling us to conqueror all that life presents.

The fundamental truth as it relates to all we experience in life is seen in God's provision for his children, and in his binding commitment to us. Paul captures these thoughts in his concluding verses of this chapter. And so, wherever we find ourselves right now, let's read aloud these powerful words – affirming, with the apostle, God's truth for us all:

No, in all these things we are more than conquerors through him who loved us. For I am convinced that neither death nor life, neither angels nor demons, neither the present nor the future, nor any powers, neither height nor depth, nor anything else in all creation, will be able to separate us from the love of God that is in Christ Jesus our Lord (vv 37-39).

Hallelujah!

Angel Food

Men ate the bread of angels; he sent them all the food they could eat (v 25).

Asaph begins this psalm by telling the people to listen up! He was about to remind them, and us, of God's kindness and faithfulness – to be passed on to the generations who would follow. As God has been with his people in the past, so he will be with us in the present:

> *O my people, hear my teaching; listen to the words of my mouth … I will utter hidden things, things from of old … we will tell the next generation (vv 1, 2, 4).*

I read in a newspaper of a mother who has a very sick little girl. Seventeen-month-old Abby has a rare congenital heart defect, and has already had three open-heart operations. Yet Abby always has a smile – evidenced by her beaming face in the picture shown in the article. Her condition, however, is extremely serious. Because Abby's mom is so thankful for each day she has her daughter, she daily does a random act of kindness – such as dropping a five-dollar bill on the street with a note attached: 'Buy yourself a little something to eat and enjoy!' Angel food.

The psalmist reminds us that God also is kind, providing for us daily – just as he did for his people in the Sinai desert centuries ago. The manna was 'the bread of angels' to sustain them; to keep them going; to give them a sense of hope – all because of God's great love.

Little Abby's mom has hope for her daughter, which makes her want to do something for others on a daily basis. God wants to shower *us* with his blessings daily by giving us spiritual food: fellowship with others; the privilege of reading his Word; communion with him in prayer. The 'food' of angels – and more! Let's take time to receive from him, be fed by him, right now.

ACTION

Think of an act of kindness you can do for at least one person today. It will bless them, bless you, and will surely bless the Lord!

There is a Redeemer

I know that my Redeemer lives (v 25).

The words and music for our song today are by Melody Green, first sung by her husband, Keith Green, in the 1980s. Keith, born in 1953, was a wonderful musician and songwriter himself. But, when only 28 years old, he tragically died in a plane crash, along with two of his little children. Keith is now *with* his Redeemer. But, when writing this beautiful song, little did he know that he would *see* his Redeemer at such a young age – and at the same time introduce his beautiful children to his precious Jesus.

The name of Jesus is above *all* names. Why? Because he died for you and for me – sinners, saved by grace:

> Jesus, my Redeemer, Name above all names,
> Precious Lamb of God, Messiah, O for sinners slain.
> (*SASB* 204 v 2)

One day we will stand in Glory with all those who have gone before us – and we'll see our Redeemer's face! Are we ready for Heaven? Keith Green had no idea when he boarded the plane that it would be his last day on earth. But from all we know of him and his vibrant ministry, he was ready and prepared to see Jesus. How important it is that we be *ready*, for no one knows the day or time when God will call us Home to be with him. However, the work on earth still needs to be done – *now*; and it will prepare us for serving our King for ever in Glory.

Let's join our voices in singing this song's refrain, thanking God for his Son, Jesus Christ, and also thanking him for his Holy Spirit – who enables us to do service for him:

> Thank you, O my Father, For giving us your Son,
> And leaving your Spirit Till the work on earth is done.[11]

Beautiful

He has made everything beautiful in its time (v 11).

Beautiful! When you hear or read this word, what images pop into you mind right away? Perhaps the sight of a brand new baby. A stunning rose. A gorgeous sunrise or sunset. A majestic mountain range. A rainbow after the rain. All so very beautiful.

Solomon goes on to tell us of something even more wonderful. That when we go through perhaps a period of great difficulty, God is present to work it through with us; and eventually he reveals to us that he has made even *that* experience beautiful – all 'in its time'. In other words, we will see beauty in everything we go through, eventually. See it as being *beautiful*. It takes trust and patience; it takes great faith in the Almighty.

Solomon then speaks about something else that's truly beautiful:

He has also set eternity in the hearts of men (v 11).

Although Ecclesiastes was written thousands of years ago, it could have been written yesterday! For it is relevant, yes even for 2016. The book itself makes us stop from our extremely busy lives, and simply *think*. To marvel at who God really is, and how he can make a transforming and eternal difference to those who accept Christ as Lord and Saviour. To know, for certain, that we are loved and valued and are given hope for our days to come. Solomon writes:

… this is the gift of God (v 13).

Our key verse for today (v 11) is definitely one of my favourites in all of Scripture. It gives me such great hope – for the present and for the future. All things *will* work out in the end, because God walks with me. And, if I prove to be faithful to him, I will one day see the eternal within me become a reality. *Beautiful!*

Prayer
Let your radiance, your *beauty*, be seen in me, Lord Jesus!

Come Together

Two are better than one … If one falls down, his friend can help him up. But pity the man who falls and has no-one to help him up! (vv 9-10).

Ecclesiastes is a fascinating read; interesting, in that we are virtually seeing into the mind of another. Solomon, a king noted for his great wisdom and discernment, debates with himself, and we somehow immediately identify with him on a very personal level. Many of the questions he asks and many of the statements he makes *we* have also questioned and stated. If not us, we know of people who can strongly relate to Solomon's philosophical sentiments.

Take our key verse for today. To have a good friend is so important – for everyone. To be able to share with another person. Then, when we fall down – physically, emotionally or spiritually – a friend can help us get back on our feet. What a treasure it is, the gift of friendship! A circle of friends. Companions to be there for us, and us for them. This is what community is all about. The fellowship of believers. Such a blessing!

John Lennon wrote a song called 'Come Together'. It was written for Timothy Leary as a campaign song, when he ran to be Governor of California against America's future President, Ronald Reagan, in 1969. Within seven weeks Lennon recorded the song with The Beatles – and it immediately became a hit. The lyrics speak of coming together with others for a purpose. To support one another; to stand with others – no matter what they are facing. To have others come alongside *us* in our time of need.

Yes, two *are* better than one. And more than two better still! Yet coming together with the Lord, in prayer, is best of all!

Prayer
Lord God Almighty, from around the world today we *come together* to worship you. Help us to be good friends to others. And thank you for the Friend of all friends, Jesus Christ, who walks with us – and, when we fall, picks us up again. Bless you, my *dearest* Friend!

You're Richer than you Think

Whoever loves money never has money enough (v 10).

The tag line for Scotiabank, one of the major banks in Canada, is: 'You're richer than you think.' One can see it on billboards across the country, printed on handouts, heard in television advertisements. The idea behind it is that if you think you don't have quite enough, you might be surprised to learn – if you've invested your money with Scotiabank, of course – you possibly have more than you think.

I am a board member of an organisation called The Canadian Foundation for Physically Disabled Persons. It's an organisation which celebrates the achievements of those with a variety of disabilities; those who have made significant contributions to society – in sport, the arts, or other areas – despite their particular impairment.

At a recent fundraiser, where I was asked to sing the Canadian Anthem and offer a prayer of thanksgiving over the meal prepared, I noted that the guest speaker for the evening was the CEO of Scotiabank. He spoke on this very theme: that we are all richer than we might think – yes, even if we have certain disabilities. We're to take up the challenge, making the best of our lives – which more than likely will enrich the lives of many others.

Most of us are not wealthy. In fact, many people in the world have very little money. Yet, when you really think about it, we are *rich* – in that we have faith in a God who loves and cares for us. Rich because we have family and friends; enough food to keep us from starving; a roof over our head. Life is not just about money in the bank. It's about what we do with our lives that really counts.

Solomon warns us about loving money too much. For this can lead us into dangerous territory. Rather, we are to value what we *do* have, and always be willing to share it with another.

PRAYER
Lord, I *am* rich, in so many wonderful ways! Help me to appreciate all I have, and to never grumble about not having enough. Never be greedy in hoarding what I do have. Thank you for supplying me with my every need.

To God be the Glory

Brothers, my heart's desire and prayer to God for the Israelites is that they may be saved (10:1).

Paul had been addressing primarily a Gentile audience. But now he expressed his deep concern for his own people – fellow Jews. In opening up faith to *all* people, in no way was God rejecting his chosen ones. Quite the opposite. They had rejected him!

> *What then shall we say? That the Gentiles, who did not pursue righteousness, have obtained it, a righteousness that is by faith; but Israel, who pursued a law of righteousness, has not attained it. Why not? Because they pursued it not by faith but as if it were by works (9:30-32).*

Some people think all we need to do is be kind, generous, helpful. Although these things are good, Paul stresses that faith is *essential*. For then we desire to share the good news of Christ with others; to let people know that the Lord can change lives completely!

> *… how can they believe in the one of whom they have not heard? And how can they hear without someone preaching to them? And how can they preach unless they are sent? As it is written, 'How beautiful are the feet of those who bring good news!' (10:14-15).*

Are we willing to be Christ's hands and feet, taking the gospel to people and helping bring them to faith? Anticipating that people *will* come to faith, now and in days to come, Paul breaks forth into a spontaneous *doxology* (from a Greek word meaning 'brightness, radiance, splendour, glory'):

> *Oh, the depth of the riches of the wisdom and knowledge of God! How unsearchable his judgments, and his paths beyond tracing out! 'Who has known the mind of the Lord? Or who has been his counsellor?' 'Who has ever given to God, that God should repay him?' For from him and through him and to him are all things. To him be the glory for ever! Amen (11:33-36).*

Yes, to God be *all* the glory!

Therefore …

Therefore, I urge you, brothers, in view of God's mercy, to offer your bodies as living sacrifices, holy and pleasing to God – this is your spiritual act of worship (v 1).

Paul begins this powerful section of his letter by using the word 'therefore'. Because we are in debt to our divine Sovereign, having been forgiven of our sins, cleansed and restored; and because we are recipients of his grace and love, having been raised from death to life, we owe God everything!

Therefore, in response, we want to present our lives – once again – to the Lord. Lives that are 'holy and pleasing' to him. We do this by becoming 'living sacrifices'. Not dead ones, like the animals offered in Bible times, but passionately giving of ourselves in our desire to become more like Jesus. After all, sacrifice means giving the best we have to the One we love the most.

Yet we must be aware that 'living sacrifices' can roll off the altar! *Therefore*, we must be totally committed: body, mind, soul, spirit. A full surrender – refusing to conform to the world, but willing to be 'transformed' into the likeness of Christ:

Do not conform any longer to the pattern of this world, but be transformed by the renewing of your mind (v 2).

God wants to set our consecrated nature ablaze! For Christ is the flame that lights us, as living sacrifices, so we can be effective servants – a transformed people, longing to reach out to a world in desperate need of the Saviour.

Therefore, as our act of worship, let us express to the Lord our deep love for who he is, and for all he means to us this day.

Prayer
***Therefore*, O God, I offer myself to you afresh. Transform me, and make me more like Jesus!**

A Dry Crust

Better a dry crust with peace and quiet than a house full of feasting, with strife (v 1).

The secret ingredient to a fabulous meal is love! Love put into the preparation; love seen in those sitting at the table, ready to share in the meal. Whether it be two people or more, it's a blessing. But even if it's just one at the table, that individual can reflect upon others – praying for them; valuing each one that comes to mind.

In this chapter of Proverbs, Solomon begins by giving us a simple image – that of a dry crust. For ancient travellers, this would have significance. While travelling, they would not have been able to preserve food well, so relied on dried bread or dried meat to sustain them. Tasty? Probably not. Yet it was all they needed to stay alive.

The quality of a meal should take second place to the emotional environment of the household. Having an atmosphere of 'peace' must come first. And when the writer uses the word 'quiet', he doesn't mean silence but rather a sense of contentment, tranquillity, security, joy. It really doesn't matter what's on the plate in front of us; what matters is an air of harmony and sincere love.

We live in an age of greed. One person wants to outdo the person next to them. People long to be better and have more than their neighbour. All this causes hostility, selfishness and resentment – and, yes, great 'strife'.

The simplicity of a piece of 'dry crust' reminds us that God supplies *all* our needs. It's also a reminder that we are to have a thankful heart – appreciating all those we care for with a deep sense of love and gratitude. May each one of us sense God's 'peace and quiet' as we reflect upon his extravagant love for us this day.

Action
As we sit for meals today, whether with others or alone, let's thank God for all those who come to mind who we love and be content within – even if all we have before us is a dry crust of bread.

There's a Land

Then I saw a new heaven and a new earth, for the first heaven and the first earth had passed away (v 1).

Do you think much about Heaven? When someone close to us has passed on, or is in the process of dying, our thoughts very often *do* go heavenward. But on a daily basis our lives are so busy, even hectic at times. We become focused on what needs to be accomplished *today*. We will think about Heaven on another occasion, when we have more time! But perhaps if we *did* think more about Heaven, it would actually help us do all those things that need to get done more effectively. For our Lord is preparing a spectacular place for us – right now!

> There's a land that is fairer than day And by faith we can see it afar;
> For the Father waits over the way To prepare us a dwelling place there.
> (*SASB* 552 v 1)

Sanford Fillmore Bennett, living in the 19th century, was converted during a Methodist revival in the United States. Although a doctor of medicine, he loved to write prose and verse. One day, Joseph P. Webster – a music teacher – came by, looking quite downcast. When Bennett asked what was troubling him, Webster replied: 'It will be all right by and by.' Bennett took this thought, wrote the words of this song, gave them to Webster to compose a melody, and within half an hour they sang their completed song for friends!

When we *all* get to Heaven, we will be full of such praise and thankfulness, for God has loved and blessed us all in so many wonderful ways. We will rejoice, *together*! As we wait for that day to come, let us sing – from all around the world – this final verse and refrain, in great anticipation:

> To our bountiful Father above We will offer the tribute of praise
> For the glorious gift of his love And the blessings that hallow our days.
>   In the sweet by-and-by
>   We shall meet on that beautiful shore.

Satisfaction

All man's efforts are for his mouth, yet his appetite is never satisfied (v 7).

Solomon made wealth and self-gratification the two goals of his life. He constantly strived to prove to himself that with such aims he could satisfy his innate desire for a significant existence. But the gifts bestowed to him by God – wisdom and discernment, riches and honour (see 1 Kings 3:12-13) – could never satisfy without the *Giver*. If only Solomon had walked closely with God, he *would* have found what he had so longed for in life.

What brings *us* satisfaction? Our Scripture verse speaks of the mouth. Yet people's desires – whether it's food, money, or other 'satisfactions' – are often insatiable. Always wanting more and more. Unless God's peace and the sense of hope he brings are deep down in our being, we will never experience true satisfaction.

Some things are good and *do* bring temporary satisfaction: family, friends, work, home, ministry. And yes, even a good meal! But anything without God at the centre is virtually meaningless:

> *… a chasing after the wind (v 9).*

We close today with a prayer by theologian Dietrich Bonhoeffer, who found deep satisfaction in Christ – even knowing of his impending death at the hands of the enemy near the end of the Second World War. May these words bring us all genuine *satisfaction* in being Christ's child – no matter what lies before us.

PRAYER

O God, early in the morning I cry to you. Help me to pray and to concentrate my thoughts on you: I cannot do this alone. In me there is darkness, but with you there is light; I am lonely, but you do not leave me; I am feeble in heart, but with you there is help; I am restless, but with you there is peace. In me there is bitterness, but with you there is patience; I do not understand your ways, but you know the way for me … Restore me to liberty, and enable me to live now that I may answer before you and before me. Lord, whatever this day may bring, your name be praised.[12]

Wisdom

… wisdom preserves the life of its possessor (v 12).

My daughter Kirsten is a flight attendant. Before any plane takes off, she is obliged to inform the passengers of safety precautions. If there develops a need for oxygen, masks will fall down from a compartment above. She will then say: 'If you have a child with you, make sure you secure your own mask first, before putting the mask on your child.' I have often thought if it were me in that situation, I would probably want to make sure my child had oxygen first, before me. However, if we ourselves become disoriented – which could happen – then we are no good to another passenger. Both suffer. Wise words. Wisdom.

A definition I recently came across states that wisdom is the God-given ability to see life with rare objectivity and to handle life with rare stability. Profound! We might think we do not possess the gift of wisdom. After all, we've made bad choices in the past – proving not to be very wise at all. Solomon says:

Wisdom makes one wise man more powerful than ten rulers in a city (v 19).

It's not that we crave power. But we are to long for wisdom, in order to make good decisions in life – then be willing to help *others* do likewise. Wisdom helps us balance our lives; to live wholesome, godly lives; to give perspective for today, and for tomorrow. Wisdom helps to bring strength in our time of weakness. When people criticise us, put us down, even question our motives, wisdom helps us respond in an appropriate way. Solomon writes:

'I am determined to be wise' (v 23).

As we show the face of God's wisdom – and breathe in godly insight – may we treasure this precious gift. For wisdom helps us navigate through life, reflecting the beauty of Jesus in all we do and say:

Wisdom brightens a man's face and changes its hard appearance (8:1).

Let the *glow* on our faces today reflect God's beauty in us!

Clothed in White

All share a common destiny – the righteous and the wicked, the good and the bad, the clean and the unclean (v 2).

We will all die. We are mortal. Our lives *will* come to an end on earth – 'under the sun' (v 3). But for believers in Christ Jesus, death here means life to come. A new beginning – that will last *for ever*! Solomon tells us, then, that we are to enjoy life to the full:

Go, eat your food with gladness, and drink your wine with a joyful heart, for it is now that God favours what you do. Always be clothed in white, and always anoint your head with oil (vv 7-8).

We're never to be frivolous with the life God has given to us. But we are to be 'clothed in white', our heads anointed with oil. A life of purity. Holy lives. Undefiled. And having 'a joyful heart' – for we're so blessed.

Solomon then reminds us to be useful and effective:

Whatever your hand finds to do, do it with all your might (v 10).

Many of us come up with good ideas, having good intentions to see them through. But unless we put those thoughts into action, it is fruitless. When opportunities arise – that will benefit ourselves and others, and will glorify God – then we must act upon them. For we have no time in which to live but the present; the past is gone, and the future has not yet come. It might take effort, but our motive for moving forward lies in our deep love for God. To serve him well.

Our destiny goes far beyond this life. We will soon all be going *Home*. Let us end life on earth as best we can, living as God would have us do – in preparation for our *eternal* life, with him, in Glory!

Prayer
Clothe me in *white*, I pray, Lord. Help me to be holy, and keep me faithful; to be the very best for you now – in great anticipation for what is to come.

What the World Needs Now

Be devoted to one another in love. Honour one another above yourselves (v 10 NIV2011).

Just imagine what the world would be like if everyone loved well! People *devoting* themselves to one another; *honouring* each other above self. It must begin with us. Being sincere in our care and love for others. Putting love into action:

> *Be joyful in hope, patient in affliction, faithful in prayer. Share with the Lord's people who are in need. Practise hospitality ... Live in harmony with one another (vv 12-13, 16 NIV2011).*

After writing more on this very subject of love, Paul concludes this portion of Scripture by urging us:

> *Do not be overcome by evil, but overcome evil with good (v 21 NIV2011).*

In 1965 Hal David wrote the lyrics, and Burt Bacharach the music, for 'What the World Needs Now is Love'. The song instantly became extremely popular and has been recorded by many artists over the years. Why such success? Because people intuitively knew that genuine love for one another *can* make a huge difference. In a world where there exists so much hatred, war, crime and even terror, the notion of true love being expressed by people brings a great sense of relief – and such a blessing for all concerned.

The defining words of Hal David's powerful song are these:

> What the world needs now is love, sweet love,
> It's the only thing that there's just too little of ...

Yes, we need love. Sweet love. *God's* love! After all, only *he* can truly make the world a better place.

PRAYER
Lord, I want to love well! Let a better world begin with me.

A Holy Kiss

Greet one another with a holy kiss (16:16).

When Paul encourages believers to give each other the special greeting of God's people, it is not the kiss itself that really matters; it's the *spirit* of a 'kiss' that is crucial – lifting one another up in highest regard, so none will fall. In chapter 14 we are commanded to refrain from doing anything that could cause someone to stumble:

> *It is better not to eat meat or drink wine or to do anything else that will cause your brother to fall (14:21).*

Certain people are strong; others are weaker and can be easily swayed – resulting in yielding to temptation, slipping into failure and sin. Paul emphasises that we must support one another, willing to make sacrifices for the sake of a brother or sister in Christ. It's all about loving *well*. Putting God first, in all things – including the care for others. Samuel Logan Brengle, one of The Salvation Army's great pioneers, wrote:

'We may be gifted in speech and song as are the angels; we may be shrewd and far-seeing and able to forecast the future; we may have a wide knowledge of many subjects; we may have a mountain-moving faith; we may be charitably inclined, and feed and shelter many of the poor to the extent of using up all our resources and wearing out our bodies; but if we have not the gentle, holy, humble, long-suffering, self-forgetful, unfailing, unsuspicious, self-sacrificing, generous, lowly love of Jesus, we are nothing.'[13]

The apostle closes this powerful letter with a benediction, a doxology, for us all. As we read it together, may our hearts be lifted heavenward, giving God all the glory he so rightly deserves:

> *Now to him who is able to establish you by my gospel and the proclamation of Jesus Christ, according to the revelation of the mystery hidden for long ages past, but now revealed and made known through the prophetic writings by the command of the eternal God, so that all nations might believe and obey him – to the only wise God be glory for ever through Jesus Christ! Amen (16:25-27).*

Revive Us!

… revive us, and we will call on your name (80:18).

Psalm 79 begins with an expression of deep sorrow. Asaph was a patriotic poet who consistently wrote about the history of his nation. Their land had been invaded once again. So he pleads for God's intervention, for the people were going through an extremely difficult time:

> *We are objects of reproach to our neighbours, of scorn and derision to those around us (79:4).*

He wanted the Lord to *revive* his people, giving them a sense of hope and purpose, and the assurance of his presence:

> *Then we your people, the sheep of your pasture, will praise you for ever; from generation to generation we will recount your praise (v 13).*

Do you ever feel defeated? I know, at times, I do. People seemingly attacking us, causing such distress. Or we sense a feeling of physical weakness, being emotionally drained. Burnt out. Down. At times, feeling 'invaded' by the enemy – to the point of crying out to God for help because we know we just cannot make it in our own strength.

In Psalm 80, Asaph continues with the same theme of defeat, of helplessness, crying out to God once again:

> *Restore us, O God; make your face shine upon us (80:3).*

We need restoration, daily; to be *revived*. Only God can do this: for our congregations; for ourselves individually. Will we ask God to revive us, right now, so we can be effective for him?

PRAYER

Lord, sometimes I get discouraged with all that's going on around me. Revive me, I pray! Shine upon *me* – so I can reflect your beauty.

Jesus, Saviour, Pilot Me

The disciples went and woke him, saying, 'Lord, save us! We're going to drown!' (v 25).

They were so afraid! Jesus rebuked his disciples first, telling them how little faith they had in him. Then he rebuked the winds and the waves – creating a perfect calm. When the storms of life come upon us, we need to always call upon the Lord, in faith, to 'pilot' us:

> Jesus, Saviour, pilot me Over life's tempestuous sea;
> Unknown waves before me roll, Hiding rocks and treacherous shoal;
> Chart and compass come from thee, Jesus, Saviour, pilot me.
>
> *(SASB 655 v 1)*

Edward Hopper, living in the 19th century, was a gentle and well-educated man. His most fruitful ministry was with sailors at the small Church of the Sea and Land in the New York harbour area, where he ended up ministering until his death. Although he wrote our hymn for today especially for those sailors, it relates to everyone – for we *all* need the Lord's guidance and his stillness when trials come upon us:

> As a mother stills her child, Thou canst hush the ocean wild.
> Raging waves obey thy will When thou say'st to them: Be still.
> Wondrous Sovereign of the sea, Jesus, Saviour, pilot me.
>
> *(v 2)*

When Hopper died at the age of 70, this tribute was given at his funeral: 'Suddenly the gentle, affectionate spirit of Edward Hopper entered the heavenly port, as he had requested – safely piloted by that never-failing friend, Jesus, whose driving voice was still tenderly whispering to him, "Fear not, I will pilot thee."'

May we know that God will pilot *us*, daily – until we 'near that shore':

> When at last I near the shore, And the fearful breakers roar
> 'Twixt me and the peaceful rest, Then, while leaning on thy breast,
> May I hear thee say to me: Fear not, I will pilot thee.
>
> *(v 3)*

Robin Redbreast

I have seen slaves on horseback, while princes go on foot like slaves (v 7).

Sometimes things appear to be upside down. We expect something to be a certain way, but somehow it gets flipped – and it's hard to explain. Nobodies arrogantly take up the most prominent positions – on 'horseback' – seemingly high and mighty. While others, who have worked hard and have been so diligent in all they do, 'go on foot like slaves'. It doesn't seem fair at all!

Solomon reminds us in a rather obscure way that we must trust in the providence of God. Even though the world at times seems in disarray, God *will* work it all out – in his time. As Jesus said:

> *'But many who are first will be last, and many who are last will be first'* (Matthew 19:30).

We have a choice to make. We can either wallow in the injustices and inequalities of life; or we can take the high road – doing the best we can with what life has given us. After all, our lives are dedicated to the Lord, to be lived only for his glory.

There's a beautiful little legend by a Swedish author relating to the robin. Part of it reads as follows:

> 'But little by little he gained courage, flew close to him, and drew with his little bill a thorn that had become embedded in the brow of the Crucified One. And as he did this there fell on his breast a drop of blood from the face of the Crucified One – it spread quickly and floated out and coloured all the little fine breast feathers. Then the Crucified One opened his lips and whispered to the bird: "Because of thy compassion, thou hast won all that thy kind have been striving after, ever since the world was created."'[14]

No matter how disconnected the world seems to be at times, I want Christ's imprint on my life – just like, in this legend, Christ's blood imprinted that robin for ever. For Jesus' blood has washed me and made me whiter than snow. May it be so for us all!

Sweet Light

Light is sweet, and it pleases the eyes to see the sun (v 7).

There is a 'kindness' campaign happening in Canada. It was initiated primarily to stop the whole phenomenon of bullying. Children of all ages were taking it out on other kids. But it's also a direct message to adults: that bullying, of any sort, will not be tolerated. Many schools across the country have signed on, mounting huge charts where kids can record their particular act of kindness – whether at school, at home, or in the community.

The idea behind this campaign is to be a 'light'; to take positive initiatives in helping create a safe, happy environment for all concerned. It's just as Solomon writes:

Be happy (v 9).

Not happy just for our own sakes, but for the sake of others.

A local newspaper, picking up on this 'kindness' movement, stated that many people have caught on. They are doing things to make the lives of others just a little bit better: helping protect the vulnerable, making meals for those not able, finding time to help at a kids' club.

Solomon writes, virtually, that when we reach out to other people, going the extra mile, we will eventually reap the benefits:

Cast your bread upon the waters, for after many days you will find it again (v 1).

As we bless, *we* will be blessed – perhaps more than we ever anticipated or imagined. What must we do then?

Follow the ways of your heart (v 9).

When our heart is in tune with the Lord, he will illumine us with spiritual light. Our eyes will be open to see the glory of God in the face of Jesus, the Light of the world. Oh yes, such sweet, sweet light!

What *is* the Meaning of Life?

Honor God and obey His Laws (v 13 NLV).

Many of us are somewhat private people. Some might accuse us of keeping secrets. We would respond that we are reserved. But a column in *The Toronto Star* stated: 'No matter how tightly you hold your secrets, Google probably knows … What you look for (on line) is way more telling than information about yourself … Any time you share personal information with a website, even in an apparently throwaway capacity, you give that site a data point that it can collate into a large picture of who you are.' Enlightening – and also, perhaps for some, rather frightening!

Throughout Ecclesiastes, Solomon questions the meaning of life – often stating how 'meaningless' it is. Yet in saying this, he is really concluding that there *is* meaning and purpose. For God is in control of everything. Solomon even begins this final chapter by stating:

Remember also your Maker (v 1 NLV).

Yes, there might be doubts; there could be questions. We will wonder about natural disasters, war, injustices, inequality, tragedy, suffering. There is so much we will never begin to comprehend. But even as Solomon shares his mind and heart with us, his secret and complex concerns relating to life itself, we also learn something about him. He believes that, most of all, God alone is to be honoured and remembered always for who he is.

So Solomon concludes his intriguing book, and we conclude this book. In closing, please allow me to pray with you:

Sovereign God, thank you for revealing yourself to us in so many wonderful ways. Thank you for being our Friend, and for allowing us to commune with you daily in prayer. Thank you for my friends around the world. I humbly ask today that you give them strength and ability to face what lies ahead. Encourage their hearts and bless them *abundantly*! All this I pray in the name of the Father, Son and Holy Spirit. Amen.

Notes

1   Max Lucado, *You'll Get Through This*, © 2013 Thomas Nelson, Nashville, Tennessee, USA.

2   William Temple, *Nature, Man and God*, © 2003 Kissinger Publishing, Montana, USA.

3   Flora Larsson, 'An Open Heart' in *My God and I*, published by The Salvation Army United Kingdom Territory © 1993 The General of The Salvation Army.

4   John Fischer, *Love Him in the Morning*, © 2004 Revell, Baker Publishing Group, Michigan, USA.

5   Bob Kilpatrick, © 1978 Bob Kilpatrick Ministries/Lorenz Publishing/Small Stone Media BV, Holland (admin. Song Solutions).

6   *100 Verses and Prayers for Successful Leaders*, © 2012 Freeman-Smith, a division of Worthy Publishing, Brentwood, Tennessee, USA.

7   Alan Redpath, *Victorious Christian Service*. First published 1958 by Revell, Westwood, USA. Reprinted 2005 by Calvary Chapel Publishing, Santa Ana, USA. Copyright © Alan Redpath. All rights reserved.

8   Chris Tomlin, Ed Cash and Jesse Reeves, © 2004 worshiptogether.com, sixsteps Music (admin. Kingswaysongs.com) Alletrop Music/Music Services (admin. Song Solutions).

9   Sarah Young, *Jesus Calling*, © 2004 HarperCollins, Nashville, Tennessee, USA.

10   Flora Larsson, 'Big Me' in *Just a Moment, Lord*, first published in 1973 by Hodder & Stoughton, London. Revised and expanded edition published in 2012 by Salvation Books, International Headquarters. © The General of The Salvation Army.

11   Melody Green, © 1982 Birdwing Music/BMG Songs Inc & Ears To Hear/EMICMP/Small Stone Media BV, Holland (admin. Song Solutions).

12   Dietrich Bonhoeffer, 'I Cannot Do This Alone' in *Best Loved Prayers and Words of Wisdom*, Martin H. Manser, © 2011 HarperCollins UK, London, England.

13   Samuel Logan Brengle, *The Soul-Winner's Secret*. First published 1900, The Salvation Army, New York, USA.

14   Selma Lagerlöf, *Christ Legends*, © 1908, Henry Holt and Company, New York, USA.

Index
May–August 2016
(as from May–August 2014)

Out but not down

Swiss band **rocks** Europe

ALL THE WORLD

ministry & mission around the world

Subscribe

Words of Life is published three times a year, in January–April, May–August and September–December. *There are four easy ways to subscribe:*

1. **Post:** complete and return the subscription form below (please note details required for Gift Subscriptions). **2. Phone:** +44 (0) 1933 445445.
3. **Online:** sar.my/wolsubu (UK), sar.my/wolsubeu (europe), sar.my/wolsubrow (rest of the world) or sar.my/wolsubgift (gift subscriptions).
4. **Visit:** your local church or high street bookshop can order copies for you.

SUBSCRIPTION FORM

Name (Miss/Mrs/Ms/Mr)..

Address...

....Postcode................................

Tel.No...email*...

Annual Subscription Rates† including postage and packaging:
UK £12.45   *Europe* £17.95   *Rest of the world* £20.95

Please send me .... copy/copies of the next three issues of *Words of Life* commencing with **May–August 2016**.

Total: £ .... I enclose payment by cheque ☐
Please make cheques payable to *The Salvation Army*

Please debit my Visa / Mastercard / Switch / Maestro card:

Card No. | | | | | | | | | | | | | | | | |

Security No. | | | | **Issue number (Switch only)** ____ **Expiry date:** __/__

Cardholder's signature: .... **Date:** ....

GIFT SUBSCRIPTION FORM

Please provide details of the recipient of your Gift Subscription below. Ensure you provide your full address and payment details in the main Subscription section above, as these are required to process payments made by credit card.

Name (Miss, Mrs, Ms, Mr)...

Address...

....Postcode................................

Send this form and any cheques to: The Mail Order Department, Salvationist Publishing and Supplies, 66–78 Denington Road, Denington Industrial Estate, Wellingborough, Northamptonshire NN8 2QH, UK, or contact your local Salvation Army church for details of your nearest territorial/command supplies department, which can order copies for you.
☐ *We would like to keep in touch with you via our mailing list. If you prefer not to receive correspondence from us, please tick this box. The Salvation Army does not sell or lease its mailing lists.*
† *Subscription rates are subject to change without notice.*